THE KINGFISHER
YOUNG PEOPLE'S
ATLAS
OF THE
WORLD

KINGFISHER
Larousse Kingfisher Chambers Inc.
95 Madison Avenue
New York, New York 10016

First edition 1997

LIBRARY OF CONGRESS CATALOGING-IN-PUBLICATION DATA
Steele, Philip.
  . The Kingfisher young people's atlas of the world / Philip Steele.
—1st American ed.
      p.   cm.
  Contents: How to use maps—Maps and map making—Earth facts
and figures—Countries of the world—The Continents.
  Summary: Introduces the places and people of the world through
maps, facts, and photographs.
  1. Children's atlases.   [1. Atlases.]   I. Title. II. Title:
Young people's atlas of the world.
G1021 .S8   1997   <G&M>
912—DC21   96-40184   CIP MAPS

ISBN 0-7534-5086-0
Printed in Spain

Produced by Miles Kelly Publishing Ltd
Designer: Smiljka Surla
Editors: Rosie Alexander, Samantha Armstrong,
   Angela Royston
Assistant Editor: Susanne Bull
Picture Research: Kate Miles, Yannick Yago

THE KINGFISHER
YOUNG PEOPLE'S
ATLAS
OF THE
WORLD

Philip Steele

Kingfisher

NEW YORK

Contents

How to use a map

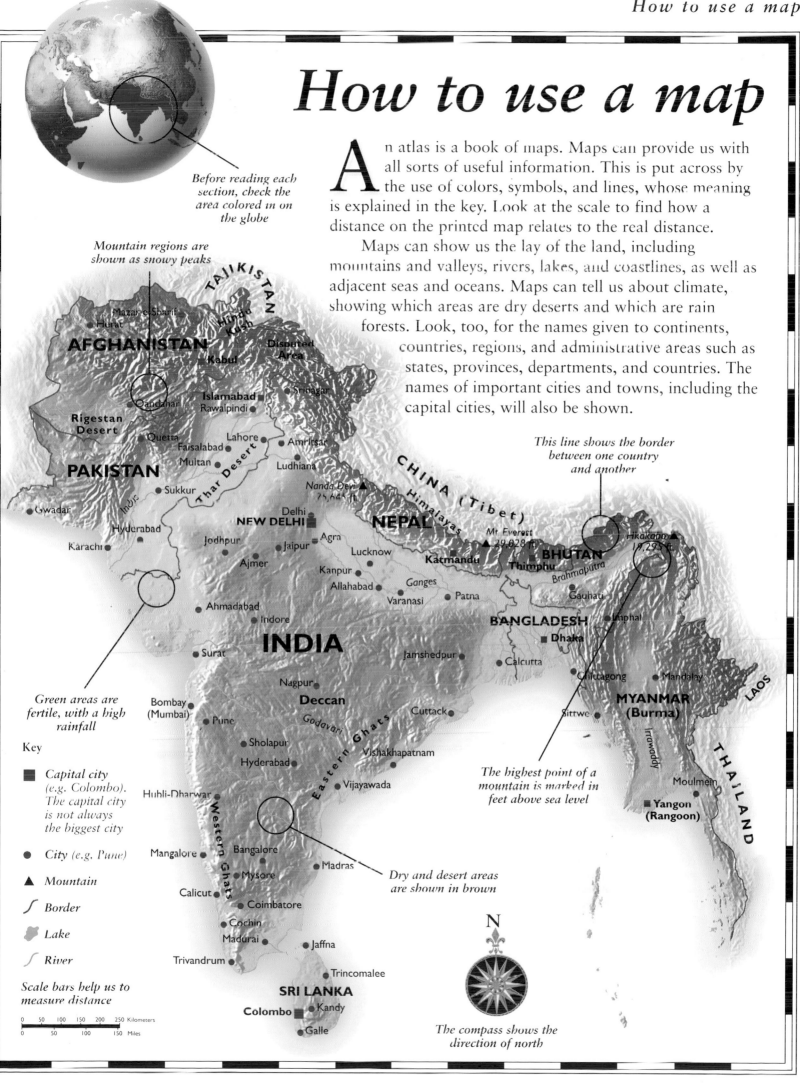

An atlas is a book of maps. Maps can provide us with all sorts of useful information. This is put across by the use of colors, symbols, and lines, whose meaning is explained in the key. Look at the scale to find how a distance on the printed map relates to the real distance.

Maps can show us the lay of the land, including mountains and valleys, rivers, lakes, and coastlines, as well as adjacent seas and oceans. Maps can tell us about climate, showing which areas are dry deserts and which are rain forests. Look, too, for the names given to continents, countries, regions, and administrative areas such as states, provinces, departments, and countries. The names of important cities and towns, including the capital cities, will also be shown.

Before reading each section, check the area colored in on the globe

Mountain regions are shown as snowy peaks

This line shows the border between one country and another

Green areas are fertile, with a high rainfall

The highest point of a mountain is marked in feet above sea level

Dry and desert areas are shown in brown

Key

- ■ Capital city (e.g. Colombo). The capital city is not always the biggest city
- ● City (e.g. Pune)
- ▲ Mountain
- ∫ Border
- ⬡ Lake
- ∫ River

Scale bars help us to measure distance

```
0   50  100  150  200  250 Kilometers
0   50      100     150 Miles
```

N

The compass shows the direction of north

Maps and mapmaking

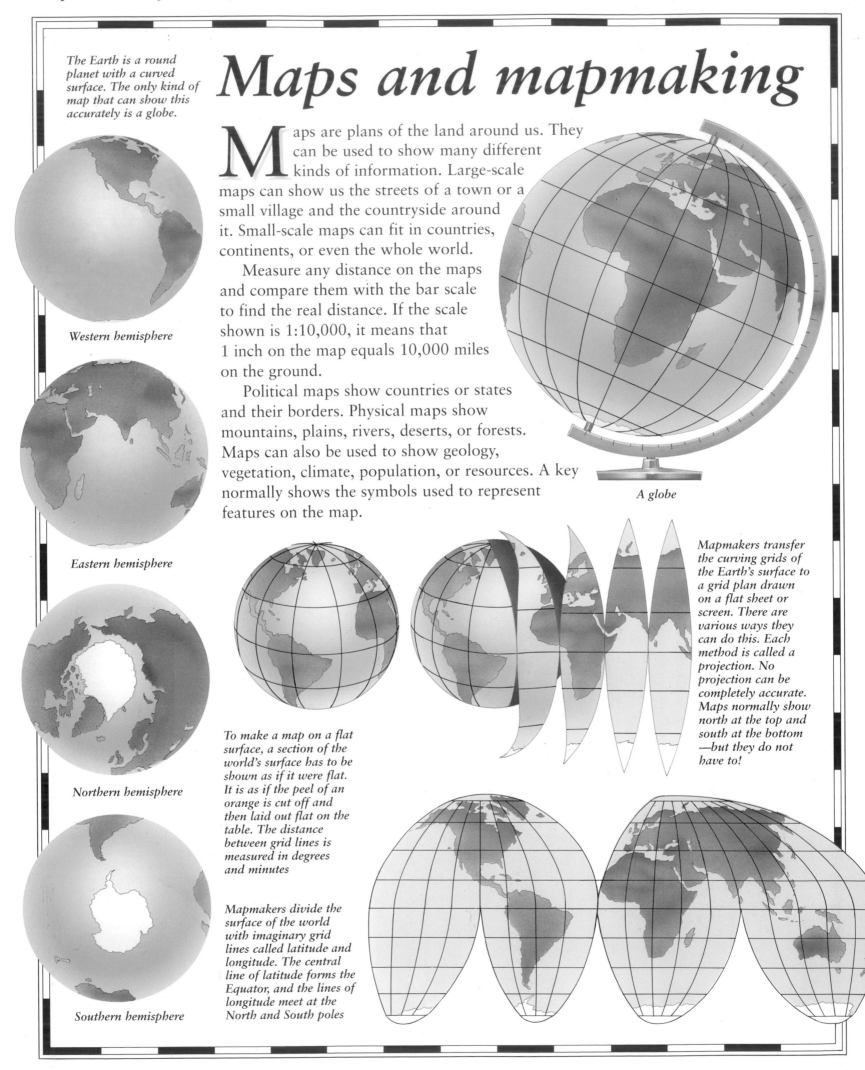

The Earth is a round planet with a curved surface. The only kind of map that can show this accurately is a globe.

Maps are plans of the land around us. They can be used to show many different kinds of information. Large-scale maps can show us the streets of a town or a small village and the countryside around it. Small-scale maps can fit in countries, continents, or even the whole world.

Measure any distance on the maps and compare them with the bar scale to find the real distance. If the scale shown is 1:10,000, it means that 1 inch on the map equals 10,000 miles on the ground.

Political maps show countries or states and their borders. Physical maps show mountains, plains, rivers, deserts, or forests. Maps can also be used to show geology, vegetation, climate, population, or resources. A key normally shows the symbols used to represent features on the map.

Western hemisphere

Eastern hemisphere

Northern hemisphere

Southern hemisphere

A globe

Mapmakers transfer the curving grids of the Earth's surface to a grid plan drawn on a flat sheet or screen. There are various ways they can do this. Each method is called a projection. No projection can be completely accurate. Maps normally show north at the top and south at the bottom —but they do not have to!

To make a map on a flat surface, a section of the world's surface has to be shown as if it were flat. It is as if the peel of an orange is cut off and then laid out flat on the table. The distance between grid lines is measured in degrees and minutes

Mapmakers divide the surface of the world with imaginary grid lines called latitude and longitude. The central line of latitude forms the Equator, and the lines of longitude meet at the North and South poles

The Earth

The Earth is a great ball of rock that spins around as it travels through space. It is one of the nine planets that, together with asteroids and comets, travel around our local star, which we call the Sun. The Sun, a fiercely hot ball of gas, provides the Earth with warmth and light. The atmosphere, a layer of gases that surrounds the Earth, shields us from some of the Sun's more harmful rays. It also provides the air that makes it possible for people to live on Earth.

PLANET EARTH

Circumference around the Equator: 24,901 miles
Circumference around the poles: 24,859 miles
Diameter at the Equator: 7,926 miles
Surface area: 196 million sq. miles
Area covered by sea: 71 percent
Average distance from the Sun: 93,000,000 miles
Average distance from the Moon: 256,667 miles
Period of rotation: 23 hours 56 minutes
Speed of rotation: 1,106 miles per hour at the Equator
Period of revolution: 365 days 6 hours
Speed of revolution: 19.87 miles per second

Earth

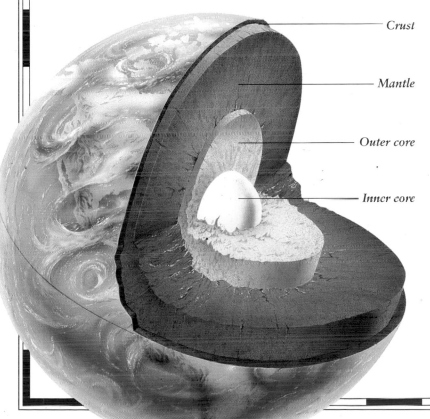

Crust

Mantle

Outer core

Inner core

HIGHEST PEAKS

Mountain	Height (feet)	Location
Everest (Qomolangma)	29,028	China-Nepal
K2 (Qogir Feng)	28,250	India-Pakistan
Kanchenjunga	28,170	India-Nepal
Makalu 1	27,766	China-Nepal
Dhaulagiri 1	26,795	Nepal
Nanga Parbat	26,657	India
Annapurna 1	26,545	Nepal
Gosainthan (Xixabangma Feng)	26,286	China
Distaghil Sar	25,869	India
Nanda Devi	25,643	India

LONGEST RIVERS

River	Length (miles)	Location
Nile	4,157	North Africa
Amazon	4,082	South America
Chang Jiang (Yangtze)	3,716	Central China
Mississippi-Missouri-Red Rock	3,741	North America
Yenisey-Angara-Selenga	3,647	Mongolia-Russia
Ob-Irtysh	3,362	Russia-Kazakhstan
Huang He	3,007	Northern China
Zaïre (Congo)	2,877	Central Africa
Lena-Kirenga	2,734	Russia
Mekong	2,597	Southeast Asia

LARGEST LAKES

Lake	Area (sq. miles)	Location
Caspian Sea	143,200	Central Asia
Superior	31,760	U.S.A.-Canada
Aral Sea	24,900	Central Asia
Victoria	21,300	East Africa
Huron	23,000	U.S.A.-Canada
Michigan	22,400	U.S.A.-Canada
Tanganyika	12,350	East Africa
Baikal	12,160	Russia
Great Bear	12,100	Canada
Malawi	8,680	Southern Africa

LARGEST ISLANDS

Island	Area (sq. miles)
Greenland	839,780
New Guinea	312,085
Borneo	292,220
Madagascar	229,355
Sumatra	202,300
Baffin	183,760
Honshu	88,955
Great Britain	88,730
Ellesmere	82,100
Victoria	81,910

MAJOR WATERFALLS

Highest	Height (feet)	Location
Angel Falls	2,648	Venezuela
Mardsalsfossen	2,540	Norway
Yosemite	1,430	United States

Greatest volume	Volume	Location
Boyoma	600,000 cu. ft. per sec.	Zaire (Democratic Republic of Congo)

OCEANS

Name	Area (sq. miles)
Pacific	63,838,000
Atlantic	31,736,000
Indian	28,364,000
Arctic	5,426,000

Countries of the World

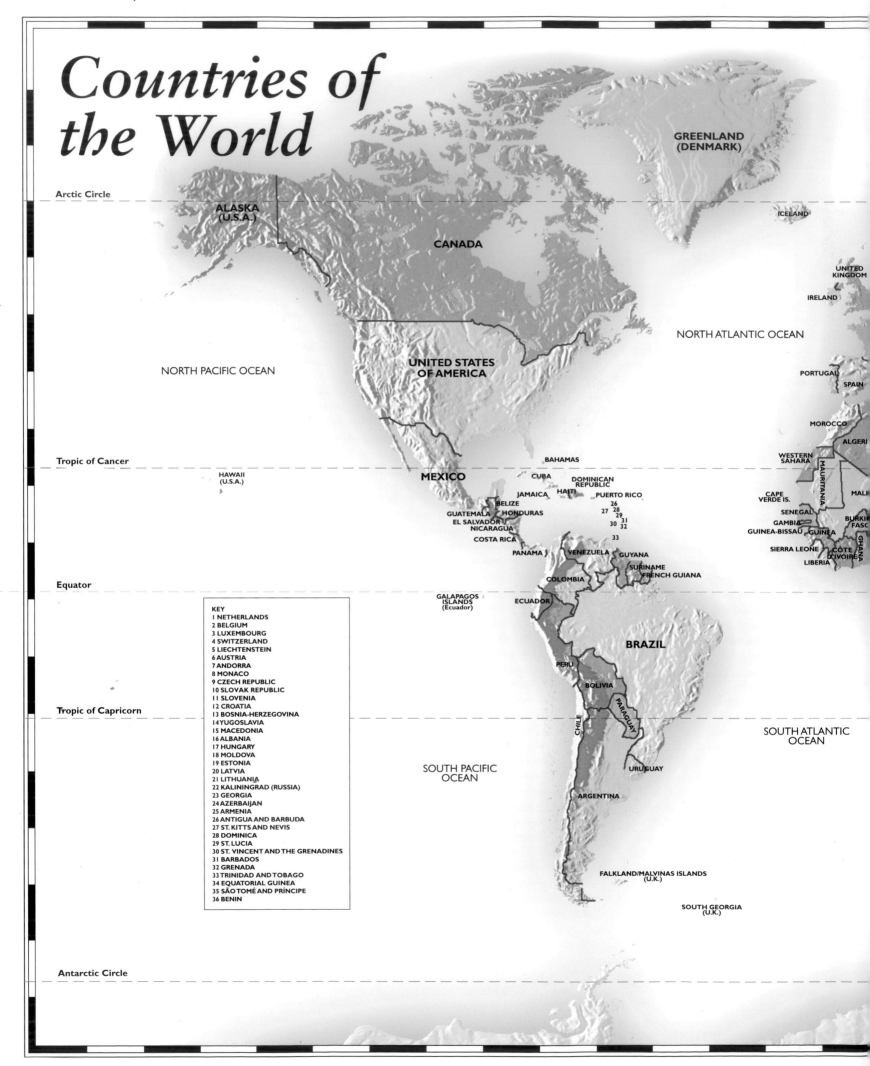

GREENLAND
(DENMARK)

Arctic Circle

ALASKA
(U.S.A.)

ICELAND

CANADA

UNITED
KINGDOM

IRELAND

NORTH ATLANTIC OCEAN

NORTH PACIFIC OCEAN

UNITED STATES
OF AMERICA

PORTUGAL

SPAIN

MOROCCO

ALGERI

Tropic of Cancer

WESTERN
SAHARA

HAWAII
(U.S.A.)

BAHAMAS

MEXICO

CUBA

DOMINICAN
REPUBLIC

JAMAICA HAITI

PUERTO RICO

BELIZE

26

GUATEMALA HONDURAS

27 28

EL SALVADOR

29

NICARAGUA

30 31
32

COSTA RICA

33

CAPE
VERDE IS.

MAURITANIA

MALI

SENEGAL

BURKII
FASC

GAMBIA

GUINEA-BISSAU GUINEA

GHANA

SIERRA LEONE

CÔTE
D'IVOIRE

LIBERIA

PANAMA

VENEZUELA GUYANA

SURINAME

COLOMBIA

FRENCH GUIANA

Equator

GALAPAGOS
ISLANDS
(Ecuador)

ECUADOR

KEY
1 NETHERLANDS
2 BELGIUM
3 LUXEMBOURG
4 SWITZERLAND
5 LIECHTENSTEIN
6 AUSTRIA
7 ANDORRA
8 MONACO
9 CZECH REPUBLIC
10 SLOVAK REPUBLIC
11 SLOVENIA
12 CROATIA
13 BOSNIA-HERZEGOVINA
14 YUGOSLAVIA
15 MACEDONIA
16 ALBANIA
17 HUNGARY
18 MOLDOVA
19 ESTONIA
20 LATVIA
21 LITHUANIA
22 KALININGRAD (RUSSIA)
23 GEORGIA
24 AZERBAIJAN
25 ARMENIA
26 ANTIGUA AND BARBUDA
27 ST. KITTS AND NEVIS
28 DOMINICA
29 ST. LUCIA
30 ST. VINCENT AND THE GRENADINES
31 BARBADOS
32 GRENADA
33 TRINIDAD AND TOBAGO
34 EQUATORIAL GUINEA
35 SÃO TOMÉ AND PRÍNCIPE
36 BENIN

BRAZIL

PERU

BOLIVIA

PARAGUAY

Tropic of Capricorn

SOUTH ATLANTIC
OCEAN

CHILE

SOUTH PACIFIC
OCEAN

URUGUAY

ARGENTINA

FALKLAND/MALVINAS ISLANDS
(U.K.)

SOUTH GEORGIA
(U.K.)

Antarctic Circle

0   1000   2000   3000   4000   5000   6000 Kilometers
0   1000   2000   3000   4000 Miles

ARCTIC OCEAN

RUSSIA

SWEDEN
FINLAND
NORWAY
DENMARK
19
20
22   21
BELARUS
GERMANY
POLAND
UKRAINE
9
10
17
ROMANIA
8
6   7
5
11   12
13   14
BULGARIA
16   15
GREECE
TURKEY
ITALY

KAZAKHSTAN

MONGOLIA

NORTH PACIFIC OCEAN

UZBEKISTAN
KYRGYZSTAN
TURKMENISTAN
TAJIKISTAN
23
25   24

NORTH
KOREA

SOUTH
KOREA

JAPAN

CYPRUS   SYRIA
LEBANON
ISRAEL
JORDAN
IRAQ
IRAN
AFGHANISTAN
KUWAIT
PAKISTAN
TUNISIA

CHINA

LIBYA
EGYPT
SAUDI
ARABIA
BAHRAIN
QATAR
UNITED ARAB
EMIRATES
OMAN
NEPAL
BHUTAN
BANGLADESH

TAIWAN

INDIA

NIGER
CHAD
SUDAN
ERITREA
YEMEN
MYANMAR
(BURMA)
LAOS
THAILAND   VIETNAM
CAMBODIA
PHILIPPINES

GERIA
CENTRAL
AFRICAN
REPUBLIC
ETHIOPIA
SRI
LANKA
MALDIVES

PALAU
FED STATES OF
MICRONESIA
MARSHALL
ISLANDS

KIRIBATI

34
CAMEROON
ZAIRE
(D.R.C.)
UGANDA
SOMALI REPUBLIC
CONGO
GABON
RWANDA
KENYA
BURUNDI
TANZANIA

INDIAN OCEAN

BRUNEI
MALAYSIA
SINGAPORE

SEYCHELLES

TUVALU

ANGOLA
MALAWI
COMOROS
INDONESIA
PAPUA
NEW
GUINEA
SOLOMON
ISLANDS
WESTERN
SAMOA

ZAMBIA
MOZAMBIQUE
TONGA
VANUATU
FIJI
NAMIBIA
ZIMBABWE
MADAGASCAR
MAURITIUS
RÉUNION
(FR.)
NEW CALEDONIA
(FR.)
BOTSWANA
SWAZILAND

AUSTRALIA

SOUTH
AFRICA
LESOTHO

NEW
ZEALAND

ANTARCTICA

The Continents

Arctic Circle

NORTH
AMERICA

ATLANTIC
OCEAN

PACIFIC OCEAN

Tropic of Cancer

Caribbean

Central
America

SOUTH
AMERICA

Tropic of Capricorn

Antarctic Circle

NORTH AND CENTRAL AMERICA
Land area: 9,358,000 sq. miles
Population: 454,000,000
Largest country: Canada
   (3,850,789 sq. miles)
Smallest country: Grenada
   (131 sq. miles)
Most crowded country:
Barbados (1,545 people per sq. mile)
Largest city: Mexico City (population
   20,200,000)
Highest point: Mt. McKinley (Denali)
   20,320 feet
Lowest point: Death Valley
   (282 feet below sea level)

SOUTH AMERICA
Land area: 6,875,000 sq. miles
Population: 458,000,000
Largest country: Brazil
   (3,285,620 sq. miles)
Smallest country: French Guiana
   (35,135 sq. miles)
Most crowded country: Ecuador
   (105 people per sq. mile)
Largest city: São Paulo
   (population 17,400,000)
Highest point: Aconcagua (22,834 feet)
Lowest point: Valdés, Argentina
   (131 feet below sea level)

EUROPE
Area: 4,031,866 sq. miles
Population: 692,126,000
Largest country: Russian Federation
   (European sector 1,526,946 sq. miles)
Smallest country: Vatican City
   (0.15 sq. miles)
Most crowded country: Monaco
   (42,020 people per sq. mile)
Largest city: Moscow (population
   8,800,000)
Highest point: Mount Elbrus (18,481 feet)
Lowest point: Volga delta
   (92 feet below sea level)
Longest river: Volga (2,290 miles)

N

ARCTIC

Scandinavia

EUROPE

ASIA

Middle East

AFRICA

South East Asia

ASIA
Area: 17,005,000 sq. miles
Population: 3,233,000,000
Largest country: Russian Federation
(Asian sector 5,064,158 sq. miles)
Smallest country: Maldives
(116 sq. miles)
Most crowded country: Singapore
(11,702 people per sq. mile)
Largest city: Tokyo (population
18,100,000)
Highest point: Everest (29,028 feet)
Lowest point: Dead Sea (1,286 feet
below sea level)

PACIFIC OCEAN

AUSTRALIA

AFRICA
Area: 11,700,000 sq. miles
Population: 682,000,000
Largest country: Sudan
(971,102 sq. miles)
Smallest country: Seychelles
(108 sq. miles)
Most crowded country: Mauritius
(1,430 people per sq. mile)
Largest city: Cairo (population
9,000,000)
Highest point: Kilimanjaro (19,340 feet)
Lowest point: Lac Assal, Djibouti
(512 feet below sea level)

AUSTRALIA / PACIFIC IS.
Land area: 3,300,000 sq. miles
Population: 28,000,000
Largest country: Australia
(2,967,124 sq. miles)
Smallest country: Nauru (8 sq. miles)
Most crowded country: Nauru
(1,238 people per sq. mile)
Largest city: Sydney
(population 3,700,000)
Highest point: Mt. Wilhelm,
Papua New Guinea (14,794 feet)
Lowest point: Lake Eyre (52 feet
below sea level)

ANTARCTICA

Canada

Canada is a vast country, second only to the Russian Federation in area. And yet it is inhabited by only 28 million people, and they mostly live in the far south, along the United States border. The reason is that the far north of Canada is an icy wilderness, lying within the Arctic Circle. Nearly half of the country is covered by evergreen forest. Winters are severe throughout the country, but the brief summers may be warm, even in the Arctic.

The northern wilderness is rich in minerals, oil, and gas, while the fertile prairies of the south form one of the world's most important wheat-growing regions. Cattle, timber, and fisheries are all important to the Canadian economy. Large cities such as Vancouver, Toronto, and Montreal are major industrial and business centers. Canada is a member of NAFTA (the North American Free Trade Agreement).

Most Canadians are descended from European settlers, and the two main languages spoken are English and French. A number of French Canadians want Quebec to become an independent nation. Canada also has a growing Asian population. Descendants of the first Canadians, Indian and Inuit, today number about 330,000.

The Niagara Falls lies on a strait between lakes Erie and Ontario, on the Canadian – U.S. border. Two great cascades drop over sheer cliffs in a colossal curtain of spray.

The CN Tower soars to a height of 1,821 feet above the skyline of Toronto, in Ontario. This lakeside city is the biggest in Canada, a center of international business and industries such as food processing, meat packing, engineering, and clothing.

Canada

Ships enter a system of locks as they navigate the St. Lawrence River and Seaway. This vital link, opened in 1959, gives Atlantic shipping access to the industrial cities of the Great Lakes region. Before the Seaway was built, there were several impassable rapids on the route.

Canadian Indian tribes live on the Pacific coast of North America. Tall totem poles of carved wood may be seen in their villages. They feature figures from ancient myths and legends.

ARCTIC OCEAN

Banks Island

ALASKA (U.S.A.)

Porcupine

Dawson

Great Bear Lake

YUKON TERRITORY

Mackenzie

Mt. Logan 19,524 ft.

★Whitehorse

Yellowknife

Liard

Great Slave Lake

BRITISH COLUMBIA

Peace

Prince Rupert

Peace River

ALBERTA

Mt. Robson 12,972 ft.

Rocky Mountains

Edmonton★

N. Saskatchewan

Princ Albe

Fraser

Vancouver Island

Calgary

Saskatoon

Vancouver

Medicine Hat

Victoria ★

S. Saskatchewan

NORTH PACIFIC OCEAN

UNITED STATES O

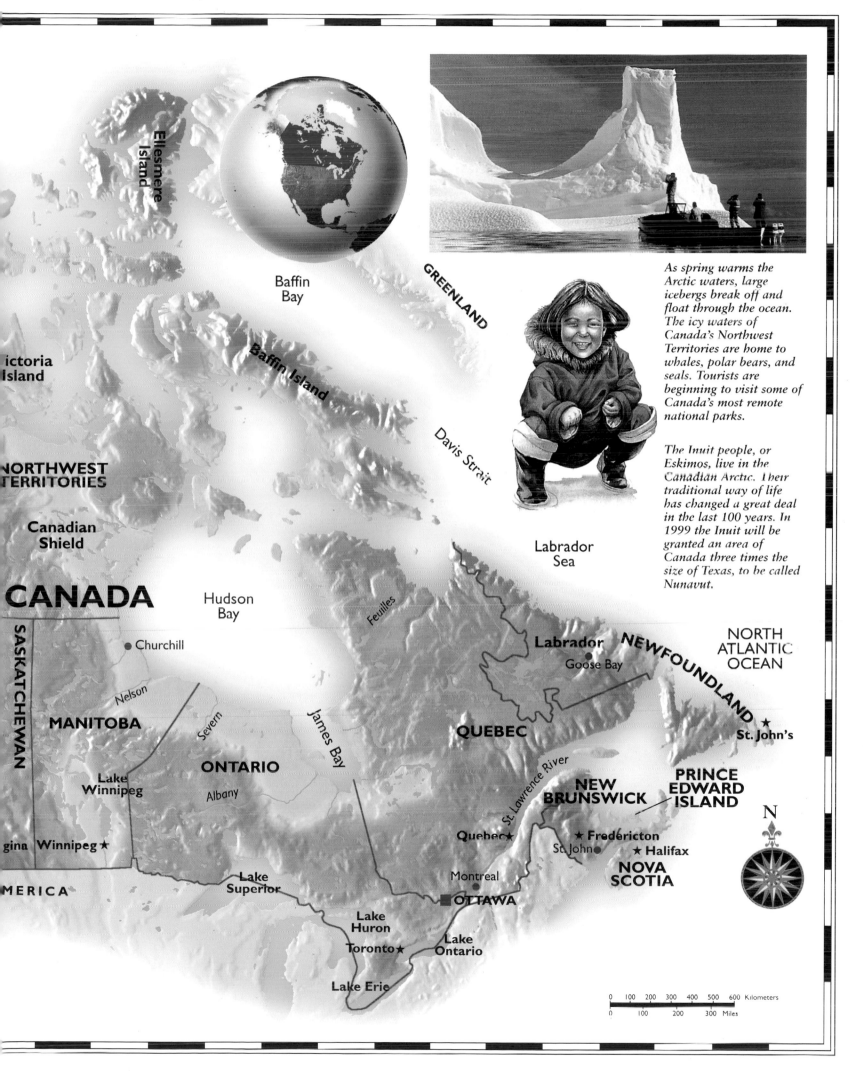

Ellesmere Island

Baffin Bay

GREENLAND

Victoria Island

Baffin Island

NORTHWEST TERRITORIES

Canadian Shield

Davis Strait

Labrador Sea

CANADA

Hudson Bay

Feuilles

Labrador

NEWFOUNDLAND

NORTH ATLANTIC OCEAN

SASKATCHEWAN

• Churchill

Goose Bay

Nelson

MANITOBA

Severn

James Bay

QUEBEC

St. John's ★

Lake Winnipeg

ONTARIO

Albany

St. Lawrence River

NEW BRUNSWICK

PRINCE EDWARD ISLAND

gina Winnipeg ★

Quebec ★

★ Fredericton

St. John ● ★ Halifax

Montreal

NOVA SCOTIA

Lake Superior

■ OTTAWA

Lake Huron

Toronto ★

Lake Ontario

AMERICA

Lake Erie

N

As spring warms the Arctic waters, large icebergs break off and float through the ocean. The icy waters of Canada's Northwest Territories are home to whales, polar bears, and seals. Tourists are beginning to visit some of Canada's most remote national parks.

The Inuit people, or Eskimos, live in the Canadian Arctic. Their traditional way of life has changed a great deal in the last 100 years. In 1999 the Inuit will be granted an area of Canada three times the size of Texas, to be called Nunavut.

| 0 | 100 | 200 | 300 | 400 | 500 | 600 | Kilometers |

| 0 | 100 | 200 | 300 | Miles |

United States of America

The United States of America stretches a third of the way around the Earth, crossing eight time zones. It occupies the center of the North American continent, lying between the North Atlantic and the North Pacific oceans. It also takes in Alaska, far to the north, and the distant Hawaiian islands, in the Pacific Ocean. The U.S.A. is divided into 50 states, each one represented by a star on the national flag.

Land and climate vary hugely, encompassing Arctic wilderness, the burning deserts of the Southwest, the northern forests and southern swamps, great chains of mountains, and the rolling grasslands called prairies. The western state of California lies within an earthquake zone, and the Hawaiian islands have volcanic eruptions. In parts of the U.S.A. there are great cities of gleaming skyscrapers and sprawling factories, linked by busy freeways. The U.S.A. is rich in natural resources. It produces aircraft, motor vehicles, electrical goods, and computers and is the world leader in business and finance.

PACIFIC OCEAN

The Statue of Liberty was a gift from France in 1886. It towers over New York Harbor and represents freedom for all Americans. Sightseers can climb up inside the statue and look out from the gallery under Liberty's crown.

CANADA

Seattle
Olympia★
WASHINGTON
Portland
Salem★
Cascade Range
Columbia
Helena★
Missouri
MONTANA

OREGON
Boise★
IDAHO
Snake
WYOMING
N. Platte
Cheyenne★

Great Basin
Salt Lake City★
UTAH
Carson City★
Sacramento★
San Francisco
San Jose
Coast Ranges
NEVADA
Colorado
S. Platte
Denver★
COLORADO
Arkansas

Las Vegas
CALIFORNIA
Grand Canyon
Colorado
Los Angeles
Santa Fe★
ARIZONA
NEW MEXICO
San Diego
Phoenix★
Gila
Rio Grande
El Paso
Pecos

MEXICO

Most North American wild cats live in undeveloped areas west of the Mississippi River. The jaguar was found in the Southwest up until the early 1900s, though now it is restricted to Central and South America.

United States of America

NORTH DAKOTA
★ Bismarck

SOUTH DAKOTA
★ Pierre

MINNESOTA

Lake Superior

WISCONSIN
Minneapolis
St. Paul ★
Madison ★
Milwaukee

MICHIGAN
Lake Michigan
Lansing ★
Detroit

MAINE
★ Augusta

VERMONT
Montpelier ★

MASSACHUSETTS
Lake Huron

Lake Ontario

NEW HAMPSHIRE
Concord ★

★ Boston
RHODE IS.
★ Providence

NEW YORK
Albany ★
Hartford
CONNECTICUT
Buffalo
New York City

Lake Erie
Cleveland
PENNSYLVANIA
Harrisburg
Pittsburgh
Toledo

NEW JERSEY
★ Trenton
Philadelphia

NEBRASKA
Lincoln ★

IOWA
Des Moines ★

ILLINOIS
Chicago
Springfield ★

INDIANA
Indianapolis ★
Cincinnati

OHIO
Columbus ★

WEST VIRGINIA
Charleston ★

Baltimore
★ Dover
DELAWARE
Annapolis ★
WASHINGTON D.C.
MARYLAND

Richmond
VIRGINIA

Great Plains

KANSAS
Kansas City
Topeka ★

Jefferson City ★
St. Louis

MISSOURI

Missouri

KENTUCKY
Frankfort ★

Ohio

Winston-Salem
NORTH CAROLINA
★ Raleigh

OKLAHOMA
Oklahoma City ★

ARKANSAS
Little Rock ★

Arkansas

Memphis

TENNESSEE
★ Nashville

Tennessee

SOUTH CAROLINA
★ Columbia

Red River

MISSISSIPPI
Jackson ★

Alabama

Atlanta ★

ALABAMA
Montgomery ★

GEORGIA

NORTH ATLANTIC OCEAN

TEXAS
Dallas

Brazos

LOUISIANA
Baton Rouge ★
New Orleans

Mississippi

Jacksonville

Tallahassee ★

Austin ★

Houston

Rio Grande
San Antonio

FLORIDA

Miami

Gulf of Mexico

N

0 100 200 300 400 Kilometers
0 50 100 150 200 250 Miles

17

Tens of thousands of years ago, Asia and North America were joined across what is now the Bering Strait. Over the ages, people from Siberia crossed into the Americas and moved southward. The descendants of some of these people, Native Americans, still live in the U.S.A. today. Europeans —Spanish, French, Dutch, and British— began to settle in North America in the 1500s and 1600s. They occupied ancient tribal lands and brought in African slaves to provide labor. The British colonists in the east declared their independence from British rule in 1776, forming a new republic. The new country grew and grew.

Today, many different people live in the U.S.A., including the descendants of Africans, Irish, Italians, Germans, Poles, Jews, Chinese, and Japanese. Many of these groups have kept their own traditions but are also American citizens. The rights of each citizen are guaranteed by the Constitution, which was first drawn up when the country was founded. Some U.S. laws are federal, covering the whole nation; others vary from state to state. The U.S.A. is a democracy with two main political parties, the Democrats and the Republicans. The head of state is a president, elected every four years.

ARCTIC OCEAN

Barrow
Colville
Brooks Range
Porcupine
RUSSIA
Noatak
Kobuk
Koyukuk
Fort Yukon
CANADA
Bering Strait
Nome
ALASKA
Fairbanks
Yukon
Tanana
Yukon
▲ Mt. McKinley
20,322 ft.
Alaska Range
Copper
Anchorage
Bethel
Kenai
Cordova
★Juneau
Dillingham
Seward
Homer
Sitka
Gulf of
Alaska
Ketchikan
Bering Sea
Kodiak

Aleutian Islands

PACIFIC OCEAN

Jambalaya is a spicy dish which often includes shrimp, fish, rice, green peppers, and chilies. It comes from New Orleans, Louisiana, a southern city where French influences mix with African/American.

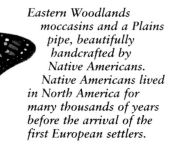

Every fall, Monarch butterflies from southern Canada and the northern United States migrate south to Mexico in huge flocks, returning the following spring.

Eastern Woodlands moccasins and a Plains pipe, beautifully handcrafted by Native Americans. Native Americans lived in North America for many thousands of years before the arrival of the first European settlers.

The bald eagle is the national emblem of the United States. Once common throughout most of North America, this powerful bird of prey became scarce as a result of poisoning by pesticides. Its numbers are now increasing and it is still common in Alaska.

The White House is the official home of the President of the United States. It is in Washington, D.C. (District of Columbia), the federal capital.

KAUAI
Kapaa
NIIHAU
OAHU
Kaneohe
Honolulu★
MOLOKAI
Kualapuu
Lahaina
LANAI
MAUI
KAHOOLAWE
Mauna Kea
13,796 ft. ▲ Hilo
HAWAII ▲ Mauna Loa
13,680 ft.

Eastern and southern states

The eastern seaboard of the United States stretches from the stormy, rocky shores of Maine down to the sunny sandbanks and islands of the Florida Keys. Inland, the long, wooded spine of the Appalachian Mountains runs north to south. To the west, the continent is crossed by the vast Mississippi–Missouri river system. This flows into the Gulf of Mexico, a warm, shallow sea fringed by swamps and steamy creeks called bayous. The huge, dry state of Texas is cattle-ranching country.

The eastern part of the United States was the first to be settled by Europeans and the first to build big industrial cities. The long and bitter Civil War was fought between northern and southern states between 1861 and 1865.

Times Square is on Manhattan Island in New York City. It lies at the heart of New York's theater district, and its bright lights advertise shows, musicals, plays, and movies.

A white church spire rises against the fall colors in Vermont, one of the six northeastern states that together make up the region known as New England. This is an area of green, wooded hills and rocky shores.

A space shuttle blasts off from the John F. Kennedy Space Center at Cape Canaveral in Florida, hitching a ride on powerful rockets. The U.S.A. has been a pioneer in space exploration. The shuttles have been used to launch satellites and to carry out scientific experiments in space.

State	Popular name	Capital	Bird	Flower	Tree
Alabama	Camellia State	Montgomery	Yellowhammer	Camellia	Southern Pine
Arkansas	Land of Opportunity	Little Rock	Mockingbird	Apple blossom	Pine
Connecticut	Constitution State	Hartford	Robin	Mountain laurel	White oak
Delaware	First State	Dover	Blue hen chicken	Peach blossom	American holly
Florida	Sunshine State	Tallahassee	Mockingbird	Orange blossom	Palmetto palm
Georgia	Empire State of the South	Atlanta	Brown thrasher	Cherokee rose	Live oak
Kentucky	Bluegrass State	Frankfort	Kentucky cardinal	Goldenrod	Tulip poplar
Louisiana	Pelican State	Baton Rouge	Brown pelican	Magnolia	Bald cypress
Maine	Pine Tree State	Augusta	Chickadee	White pine cone and tassel	White pine
Maryland	Old Line State	Annapolis	Baltimore oriole	Black-eyed susan	White oak
Massachusetts	Bay State	Boston	Chickadee	Mayflower	American elm
Mississippi	Magnolia State	Jackson	Mockingbird	Magnolia	Magnolia
New Hampshire	Granite State	Concord	Purple finch	Purple lilac	White birch
New Jersey	Garden State	Trenton	Eastern goldfinch	Purple violet	Red oak
New York	Empire State	Albany	Bluebird	Rose	Sugar maple
North Carolina	Tar Heel State	Raleigh	Cardinal	Flowering dogwood	Pine
Oklahoma	Sooner State	Oklahoma City	Scissor-tailed flycatcher	Mistletoe	Redbud
Pennsylvania	Keystone State	Harrisburg	Ruffed grouse	Mountain laurel	Hemlock
Rhode Island	Little Rhody	Providence	Rhode Island red	Violet	Red maple
South Carolina	Palmetto State	Columbia	Carolina wren	Yellow jessamine	Palmetto
Tennessee	Volunteer State	Nashville	Mockingbird	Iris	Tulip poplar
Texas	Lone Star State	Austin	Mockingbird	Blue bonnet	Pecan
Vermont	Green Mountain State	Montpelier	Hermit thrush	Red clover	Sugar maple
Virginia	Old Dominion	Richmond	Cardinal	Flowering dogwood	Dogwood
West Virginia	Mountain State	Charleston	Cardinal	Rhododendron	Sugar maple

The United States Congress meets in the Capitol in Washington D.C. The U.S.A. is a democracy. The two largest political parties are the Republicans and the Democrats.

The color and magical atmosphere of Walt Disney's cartoons are reflected in the huge Disney theme parks in California and Florida.

Between 1927 and 1941 the faces of four U.S. presidents were carved in the rockface at Mount Rushmore in South Dakota. The portraits are of George Washington, Thomas Jefferson, Theodore Roosevelt, and Abraham Lincoln. The heads, 466 feet high, are a monument to democracy.

Ninety-five percent of the state of Iowa is taken up by farmland, and most of that is given over to crops such as soybeans, corn, wheat, rye, and flax.

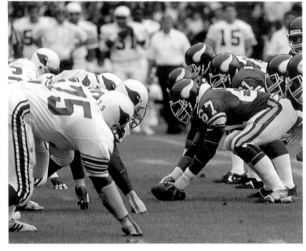

Football is a popular sport in colleges and stadiums right across the U.S.A. Players wear helmets and heavy padding for this tough, fast, contact sport which is attracting many followers in other countries.

Combine harvesters tackle huge wheat fields on the prairies. Here, the soil is rich and summers are hot. These vast grasslands form one of the world's "breadbaskets," a region upon which millions of people depend for food.

The Midwest

The Midwest stretches from the Central Lowlands around the Missouri River, westward across the High Plains to the foothills of the Rocky Mountains. Once the home of Native American buffalo-hunters, these fertile grasslands were settled by European Americans during the 1800s. The prairie grasses are taller in the wetter eastern states than in the dry shadow of the Rockies. Crops include corn and wheat, while short-grass regions are grazed by large herds of cattle or by bison, which are now protected by law. Sometimes tornadoes spin across the farmland, raising tall columns of dust. During the 1930s changes in land use and lack of rain caused large areas of farmland to become a great dustbowl. Many farmers had to give up their life on the land. Today, the prairie lands are protected from the wind by plantations of trees and are carefully conserved. There are still areas of wild prairie, many within National Park areas.

State	Popular name	Capital	Bird	Flower	Tree
Illinois	Prairie State	Springfield	Cardinal	Violet	White oak
Indiana	Hoosier State	Indianapolis	Cardinal	Peony	Tulip poplar
Iowa	Hawkeye State	Des Moines	Eastern goldfinch	Wild rose	Oak
Kansas	Sunflower State	Topeka	Western meadowlark	Sunflower	Cottonwood
Michigan	Wolverine State	Lansing	Robin	Apple blossom	White pine
Minnesota	Gopher State	St. Paul	Common loon	Pink and white lady's slipper	Norway or red pine
Missouri	Show Me State	Jefferson City	Bluebird	Hawthorn	Flowering dogwood
Nebraska	Cornhusker State	Lincoln	Western meadowlark	Goldenrod	American elm
North Dakota	Flickertail State	Bismarck	Western meadowlark	Wild prairie rose	Cottonwood
Ohio	Buckeye State	Columbus	Cardinal	Scarlet carnation	Buckeye
South Dakota	Mt. Rushmore State	Pierre	Ring-necked pheasant	Pasqueflower	Black Hills spruce
Wisconsin	Badger State	Madison	Robin	Wood violet	Sugar maple

The Grand Canyon is the biggest gorge to be found on any continent. It is about 10 miles wide and about 1 mile deep. It has been carved from the rocks of Arizona by the waters of the Colorado River. The area is a National Park.

Western and mountain states

The Rocky Mountains form a great chain, running through Canada and the United States down to Mexico. To the west of them lies a strangely beautiful landscape of salt flats, deserts, eroded rocks, and canyons. These dry lands lie in the shadow of further mountain barriers, the Sierra Nevada and the Cascade and Coast ranges. The western slopes of these mountains catch incoming Pacific rains.

The west coast enjoys a mild climate. California is warm and sunny, while Oregon and Washington are cooler and wetter. Big cities include Seattle, San Francisco, and Los Angeles, where the Hollywood district is the center of the movie industry. The region is an earthquake danger zone, and serious tremors have caused damage to Californian cities over the past 100 years.

Alaska and the Rocky Mountains are the haunt of various species of bear. The polar bear is the largest flesh-eating animal, and the Kodiak brown bear is also huge and fierce.

Grizzly bear

North American black bear

Kodiak brown bear

Polar bear

Bizarre tufa towers rim the shores of Mono Lake in California. They form when calcium in fresh water reacts with the lake water, which is three times saltier than the Pacific. The towers used to be underwater until the lake's water supply was diverted to Los Angeles and the lake became half full.

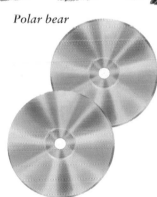

Compact discs, microprocessors, and other high-technology electronic goods are produced in California. One part of the state has been nicknamed "Silicon Valley."

Old-fashioned cable cars are a favorite sight in San Francisco. This large port, built on hills around a beautiful bay, includes wooden houses from 100 years ago in addition to modern, earthquake proof skyscrapers.

State	Popular name	Capital	Bird	Flower	Tree
Alaska	Last Frontier	Juneau	Willow ptarmigan	Forget-me-not	Sitka spruce
Arizona	Grand Canyon State	Phoenix	Cactus wren	Saguaro	Paloverde
California	Golden State	Sacramento	California valley quail	Golden poppy	California redwood
Colorado	Centennial State	Denver	Lark bunting	Rocky Mt. columbine	Colorado Blue spruce
Hawaii	Aloha State	Honolulu	Nene (Hawaiian goose)	Hibiscus	Kukui (Candlenut)
Idaho	Gem state	Boise	Mountain bluebird	Syringa	Western white pine
Montana	Treasure State	Helena	Western meadowlark	Bitterroot	Ponderosa pine
Nevada	Silver State	Carson City	Mountain bluebird	Sagebrush	Single-leaf piñon
New Mexico	Land of Enchantment	Santa Fe	Roadrunner	Yucca	Piñon
Oregon	Beaver State	Salem	Western meadowlark	Oregon grape	Douglas fir
Utah	Beehive State	Salt Lake City	Seagull	Sego lily	Blue spruce
Washington	Evergreen State	Olympia	Willow goldfinch	Western rhododendron	Western hemlock
Wyoming	Equality State	Cheyenne	Meadowlark	Indian paintbrush	Cottonwood

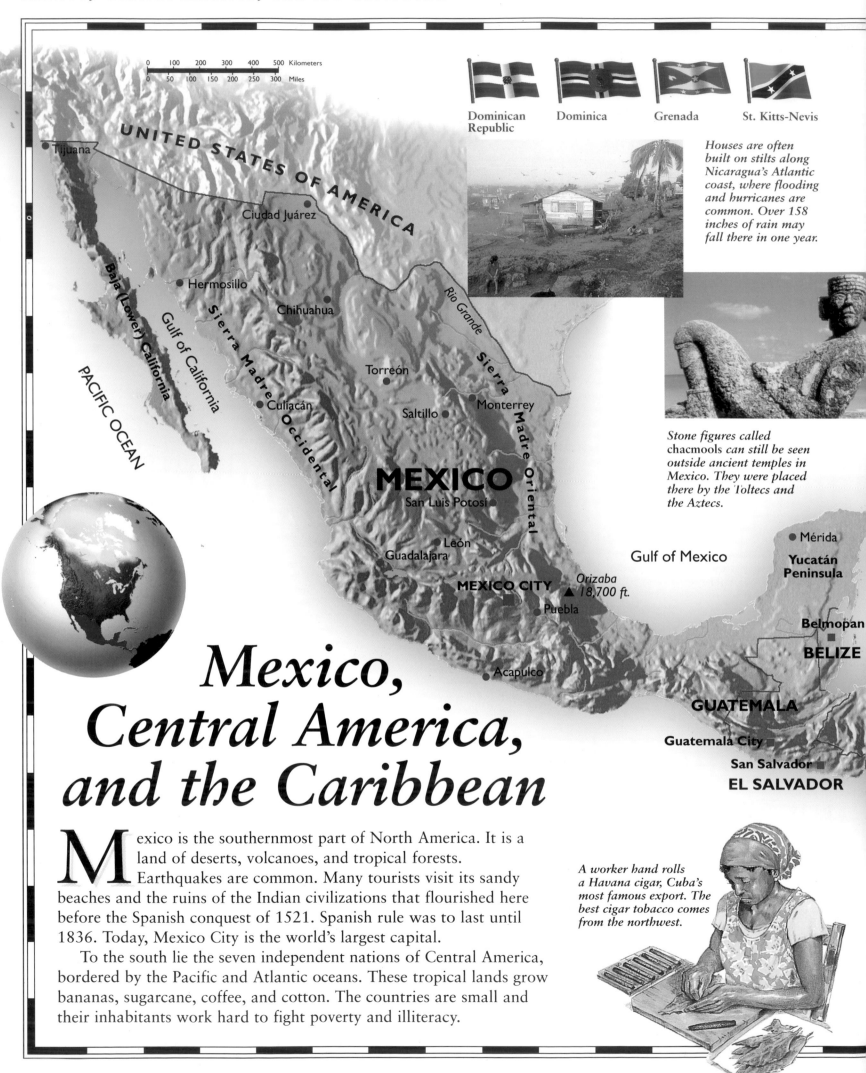

0 100 200 300 400 500 Kilometers
0 50 100 150 200 250 300 Miles

Dominican Republic   **Dominica**   **Grenada**   **St. Kitts-Nevis**

UNITED STATES OF AMERICA

Tijuana

Ciudad Juárez

Hermosillo

Chihuahua

Baja (Lower) California

Gulf of California

Sierra Madre Occidental

PACIFIC OCEAN

Torreón

Culiacán

Saltillo

Monterrey

Río Grande

Sierra Madre Oriental

MEXICO

San Luis Potosí

León

Guadalajara

MEXICO CITY   *Orizaba* ▲ *18,700 ft.*

Puebla

Acapulco

Gulf of Mexico

• Mérida

Yucatán Peninsula

Belmopan

BELIZE

GUATEMALA

Guatemala City ■

San Salvador ■

EL SALVADOR

Houses are often built on stilts along Nicaragua's Atlantic coast, where flooding and hurricanes are common. Over 158 inches of rain may fall there in one year.

Stone figures called chacmools *can still be seen outside ancient temples in Mexico. They were placed there by the Toltecs and the Aztecs.*

Mexico, Central America, and the Caribbean

Mexico is the southernmost part of North America. It is a land of deserts, volcanoes, and tropical forests. Earthquakes are common. Many tourists visit its sandy beaches and the ruins of the Indian civilizations that flourished here before the Spanish conquest of 1521. Spanish rule was to last until 1836. Today, Mexico City is the world's largest capital.

To the south lie the seven independent nations of Central America, bordered by the Pacific and Atlantic oceans. These tropical lands grow bananas, sugarcane, coffee, and cotton. The countries are small and their inhabitants work hard to fight poverty and illiteracy.

A worker hand rolls a Havana cigar, Cuba's most famous export. The best cigar tobacco comes from the northwest.

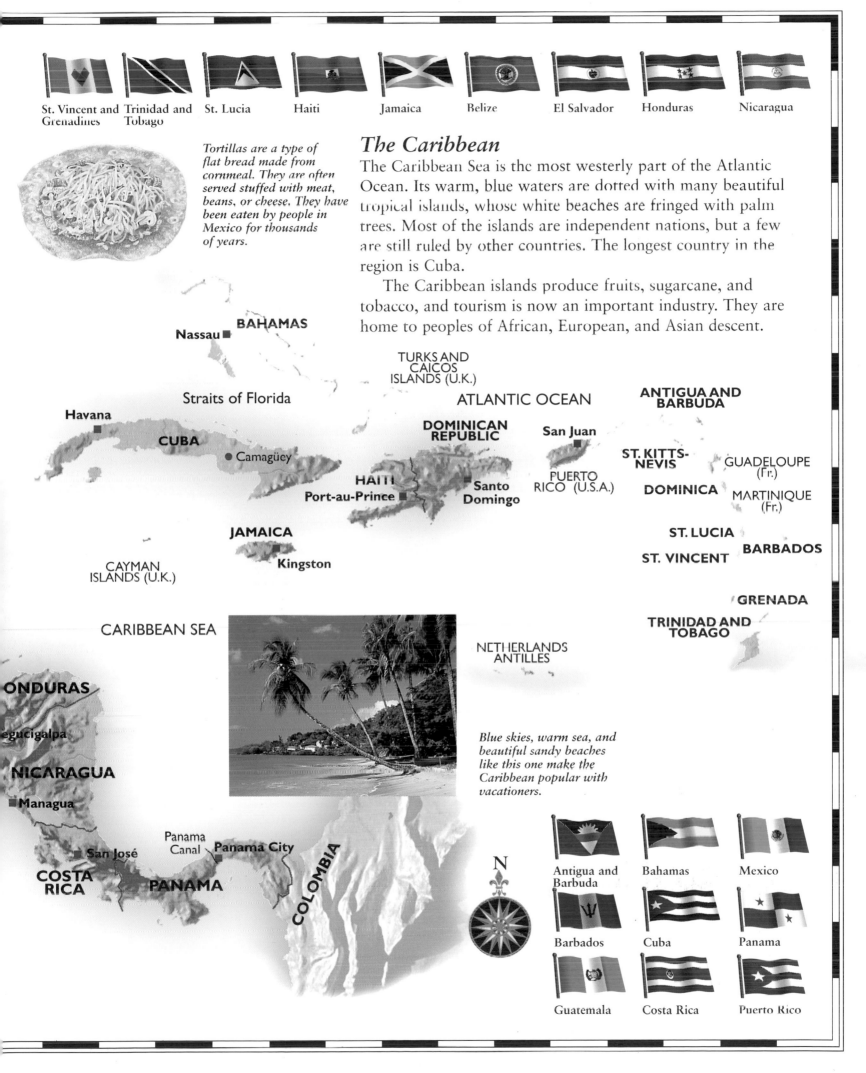

St. Vincent and Grenadines

Trinidad and Tobago

St. Lucia

Haiti

Jamaica

Belize

El Salvador

Honduras

Nicaragua

Tortillas are a type of flat bread made from cornmeal. They are often served stuffed with meat, beans, or cheese. They have been eaten by people in Mexico for thousands of years.

The Caribbean

The Caribbean Sea is the most westerly part of the Atlantic Ocean. Its warm, blue waters are dotted with many beautiful tropical islands, whose white beaches are fringed with palm trees. Most of the islands are independent nations, but a few are still ruled by other countries. The longest country in the region is Cuba.

The Caribbean islands produce fruits, sugarcane, and tobacco, and tourism is now an important industry. They are home to peoples of African, European, and Asian descent.

BAHAMAS
Nassau

TURKS AND CAICOS ISLANDS (U.K.)

Straits of Florida

ATLANTIC OCEAN

ANTIGUA AND BARBUDA

Havana

CUBA

Camagüey

DOMINICAN REPUBLIC

San Juan

ST. KITTS-NEVIS

GUADELOUPE (Fr.)

HAITI
Port-au-Prince

Santo Domingo

PUERTO RICO (U.S.A.)

DOMINICA

MARTINIQUE (Fr.)

JAMAICA

ST. LUCIA

Kingston

ST. VINCENT

BARBADOS

CAYMAN ISLANDS (U.K.)

GRENADA

CARIBBEAN SEA

TRINIDAD AND TOBAGO

NETHERLANDS ANTILLES

HONDURAS

Tegucigalpa

NICARAGUA

Managua

Blue skies, warm sea, and beautiful sandy beaches like this one make the Caribbean popular with vacationers.

Panama Canal

Panama City

San José

COLOMBIA

COSTA RICA

PANAMA

N

Antigua and Barbuda

Bahamas

Mexico

Barbados

Cuba

Panama

Guatemala

Costa Rica

Puerto Rico

The Northern Andes

The western part of South America is dominated by a long mountain chain called the Andes, which runs for 4,500 miles from north to south. In Ecuador alone there are 18 peaks rising more than 20,000 feet above sea level. To the west of the Andes, a narrow coastal plain borders the Pacific Ocean. To the east, rivers drain into the vast rain forests of the Amazon basin.

This part of South America saw the rise of great civilizations, such as the Chimú and the Inca, before the arrival of Spanish invaders in the 1530s. The region broke away from Spanish rule during the 1820s and today makes up four independent nations—Colombia, Ecuador, Peru, and Bolivia.

Many Indians, such as the Aymara and the Quechua, still live in these countries. Other inhabitants are of European or mixed descent, and Spanish is spoken throughout the region.

The area is rich in mineral resources and timber, but many people work for very low wages. Crops include corn, sugarcane, bananas, coffee, potatoes, and a grain called quinoa.

The Andean countries are famous for their finely woven blankets, ponchos, and belts. These are woven on back-strap looms, using methods that have changed little since Inca times.

These women are from La Paz, in Bolivia. La Paz is the world's highest capital city, sited at about 12,087 feet above sea level in the Andes range. The city is a center of trading in fine alpaca wool. In the cool mountain climate, these women wear woolen shawls and felt hats.

The Sun played an important role in the religion of the Incas, as this Inca Sun Festival at Sascayhuaman in Cuzco shows. The first Inca emperor was believed to be a descendant of the Sun.

This antique gold cross is studded with emeralds. Raw emeralds are found in the Andes. Huge emeralds weighing more than 16 lbs. have been found in Colombia. They have to be cut in a special way to make them sparkle.

Machu Picchu was just one town in the powerful Inca empire, which flourished about 500 years ago. Its ruins were discovered in 1911, high in the Peruvian Andes. The Incas were expert builders, engineers, farmers, and craft workers. Machu Picchu included temples and a palace. Its aqueduct channeled fresh water into the town.

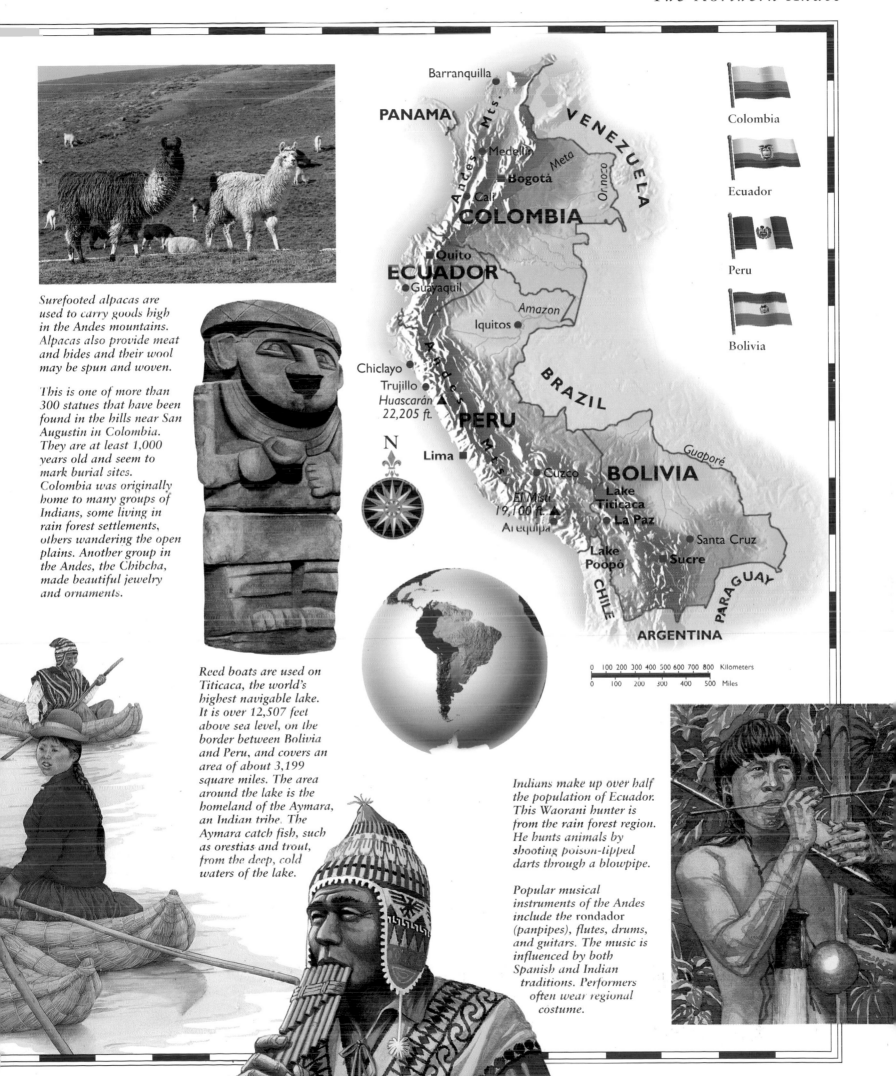

Colombia

Ecuador

Peru

Bolivia

Surefooted alpacas are used to carry goods high in the Andes mountains. Alpacas also provide meat and hides and their wool may be spun and woven.

This is one of more than 300 statues that have been found in the hills near San Augustin in Colombia. They are at least 1,000 years old and seem to mark burial sites. Colombia was originally home to many groups of Indians, some living in rain forest settlements, others wandering the open plains. Another group in the Andes, the Chibcha, made beautiful jewelry and ornaments.

Reed boats are used on Titicaca, the world's highest navigable lake. It is over 12,507 feet above sea level, on the border between Bolivia and Peru, and covers an area of about 3,199 square miles. The area around the lake is the homeland of the Aymara, an Indian tribe. The Aymara catch fish, such as orestias and trout, from the deep, cold waters of the lake.

Indians make up over half the population of Ecuador. This Waorani hunter is from the rain forest region. He hunts animals by shooting poison-tipped darts through a blowpipe.

Popular musical instruments of the Andes include the rondador (panpipes), flutes, drums, and guitars. The music is influenced by both Spanish and Indian traditions. Performers often wear regional costume.

Barranquilla

PANAMA

VENEZUELA

Andes Mts.

Medellín

Meta

Bogotá

Orinoco

Cali

COLOMBIA

Quito

ECUADOR

Guayaquil

Amazon

Iquitos

BRAZIL

Andes

Chiclayo

Trujillo

Huascarán 22,205 ft.

PERU

Mts.

N

Lima

Cuzco

BOLIVIA

Guaporé

El Misti 19,100 ft.

Lake Titicaca

Arequipa

La Paz

Santa Cruz

Lake Poopó

Sucre

CHILE

PARAGUAY

ARGENTINA

0 100 200 300 400 500 600 700 800 Kilometers

0 100 200 300 400 500 Miles

Caribbean Sea

TRINIDAD
AND TOBAGO

Caracas

Maracaibo

Orinoco

N

COLOMBIA

VENEZUELA

Georgetown

GUYANA
SURINAME

Paramaribo

Cayenne

FRENCH
GUIANA

Guiana Highlands

Orinoco

Branco

Negro

Macapá

Belèm

Japurá

Manaus

Amazon

Amazon

Madeira

Tapajós

Xingu

Tocantins

ATLANTIC
OCEAN

Fortaleza

Juruá

Purus

Araguaia

Parnaíba

Recife

PERU

São Francisco

Guaporé

BOLIVIA

BRAZIL

Salvador

Brazilian
Highlands

Mato Grosso
Plateau

BRASÍLIA

Goiânia

Belo Horizonte

PARAGUAY

Paraná

Rio de Janeiro

São Paulo

Iguaçu
Falls

Curitiba

ARGENTINA

Uruguay

URUGUAY

Pôrto Alegre

Brazil

Guyana

Suriname

French Guiana

Venezuela

*Indians lived in South
America at the time it
was conquered by Spain
and Portugal, and many
were killed or enslaved.
Today, proud of their
traditions, the Indian
tribes struggle to survive
and keep their own
lands.*

*The Kamayura are an
Indian people who live
in the Amazonian rain
forest. The men wear
feather headdresses, face
paint, and earplugs.*

*Many people in Suriname
are the descendants of
workers from Java, in
Southeast Asia. They
came to Suriname during
the years when it was
ruled by the Dutch. Here
they are performing a
traditional folk dance.*

Brazil and its neighbors

A statue in Caracas, Venezuela, honors the revolutionary hero Simón Bolívar (1783–1830). Bolívar fought for independence from Spain in the 1800s. He campaigned in Venezuela, Colombia, Peru, Ecuador, and Bolivia trying to create a federation of Spanish-speaking nations.

Brazil is the largest country in South America. It is crossed by the mighty Amazon River and a vast area of it is covered by rain forest, whose wealth of plants and wildlife is threatened as millions of trees are cut down to make way for farms and roads. Brazil also takes in grasslands and dry scrub.

To the north, Venezuela stretches from the marshes and lakes of the coast to the humid rain forests that cover the mountains in the west and south. The Orinoco River winds through the center of the country, and the grasslands of the Llanos are often flooded. Three small countries, Guyana—Suriname, and French Guiana—also lie between the highlands and the Caribbean coast.

The whole region was colonized by the Portuguese, Spanish, Dutch, British, and French from the 1500s onwards. Today it is home to many different Indian tribes, although most people are of European, African, and Asian descent.

Crops include sugarcane and coffee, and the region has many natural resources. Oil brings wealth to Venezuela, and Brazil is rich in minerals. However, many people are very poor and live in homemade shacks around growing cities such as Rio de Janeiro. Brazil is famous for its fine beaches, its carnival dances, and its love of soccer.

The red chili pod is used to make cayenne pepper, a fiery spice named after the capital of French Guiana. This is the only country in the region that is not yet independent, being an overseas department of France. French Guiana relies on its crops, but also has reserves of timber, gold, and bauxite.

Piranha fish live in many South American rivers. They have razor-sharp teeth which can rip the flesh from any animal that falls into the water in just a few seconds. Piranha fish swim in shoals numbering thousands. There are 18 species of piranha.

At Christmas in Venezuela, you may be offered halacas. *Stewed meats are put inside a pastry case made of cornflour. This is wrapped in plantain leaves and cooked in boiling water. It is usually eaten with ham and bread.*

The statue of Christ, on Corcovado peak, towers above the beautiful city and fine, natural harbor of Rio de Janeiro in Brazil.

The threatened rain forests of the tropical Amazonian Basin are a wonder of the world. Numerous species of tree, fern, and creeper grow here, and they are populated with monkeys, sloths, parrots, huge snakes, and countless insects.

Southern South America

The jagged peaks of the Andes range continue southward through the long, narrow country of Chile. This beautiful land includes one of the driest regions on Earth, the Atacama Desert on the northern coast. The southern coastline is ragged, breaking up into a maze of islands.

Paraguay lies at the heart of the continent, a hot, humid country. In its west are the thinly populated plains of the Gran Chaco; in the east are forest and grassland zones. Uruguay lies on South America's Atlantic coast above the broad estuary of the Rio de la Plata or Plate River. Its huge southern neighbor, Argentina, takes in the wide open grasslands of the Pampa. To the south lies the bleak plateau of Patagonia and Tierra del Fuego, a cold, desolate island shared with Chile.

The varied climate of southern South America means that regional produce includes very different items, such as potatoes, citrus fruits, olives, wines, sugarcane, rice, and coffee. Argentina is a major producer of beef and is famed for its cattle-ranching and its cowboys, or gauchos. Fishing is a major industry in the southern oceans. Factories manufacture cars, electrical goods, and textiles. Far out in the south Atlantic Ocean are two British territories, the Malvinas, or Falkland Islands, and the more remote islands of South Georgia. Argentina went to war with Britain over ownership of the Falklands in 1982–1983.

Buenos Aires is the capital of Argentina. It is large city and seaport on the west bank of the Plate estuary. Its name means "favorable winds."

Punta Arenas exports locally produced wool and lamb. This seaport lies in the remote south of Chile, on the Strait of Magellan. The strait provides a sea route between the Pacific and Atlantic oceans.

A statue in Montevideo commemorates the early Spanish settlers who came to build farms and ranches, crossing the land with ox-carts. Later Jesuit immigrants to southern South America included Italians, Welsh, Germans, Dutch, Poles, Hungarians, and Lebanese.

The ruined church of San Ignacio is in the province of Misiones, in northeastern Argentina. The province is named after the Jesuit missionaries who came to the region in the 1600s, with the aim of bringing Christianity to the Guaraní people.

Native American peoples living in the southern half of the continent include the Guaraní, the Mataco, and the Mapuche. The arrival of the first European settlers brought war and disease to many indigenous peoples.

This bedspread is being made out of a fine lace, known to the Guaraní people of Paraguay as ñanduti, or "spider's web." The patterns include designs of flowers, birds, and animals.

The Congress building in Buenos Aires. Argentina today is a democracy, but like many other South American countries, it has gone through long periods of military rule, dictatorship, and political unrest since it became independent from Spain in 1816.

PERU

BOLIVIA

Arica

Iquique

Antofagasta

CHILE

PARAGUAY

BRAZIL

Gran Chaco

Asunción

Tucumán

Salado

Paraná

ARGENTINA

Córdoba

Rosario

URUGUAY

Uruguay

Valparaíso

Aconcagua 22,835 ft.

Montevideo

Santiago

BUENOS AIRES

Concepción

Pampas

Mar del Plata

Colorado

Bahía Blanca

Negro

Andes

N

PATAGONIA

Chubut

SOUTH ATLANTIC OCEAN

Atacama Desert

FALKLAND ISLANDS (U.K.)

Tierra del Fuego

SOUTH GEORGIA (U.K.)

Cape Horn

| 0 | 25 | 50 | 75 | Kilometers |
| 0 | 10 | 20 | 30 | 40 | 50 | Miles |

Argentina

Chile

Paraguay

Uruguay

Maté is a hot, bitter drink that is popular in South America. It is like tea but is brewed from the leaves of a type of holly that grows in Paraguay. Traditionally it is drunk through a tube from a hollow gourd.

Scandinavia and Finland

A geyser gushes from the ground in Iceland. Geysers and warm springs are common here. Water that has seeped down through the rocks is heated by volcanic activity deep underground and forced back to the surface. Iceland has many volcanoes which still erupt from time to time.

Two claw-shaped peninsulas jut out from northern Europe. The larger one stretches south from the Arctic and takes in Sweden and Norway. It includes mountains, sea inlets called fjords, lakes, and forests. The smaller peninsula, an area of green farmland, extends northwards from Germany. Together with various islands, this makes up Denmark. The whole region is called Scandinavia.

Far to the west, in the Atlantic Ocean, is the bleak island of Iceland, which is partly covered by icefields and glaciers. Iceland was settled by Scandinavian seafarers called Vikings in A.D. 874. To the east, across the Gulf of Bothnia, the lakes and forests of Finland stretch to the Russian border.

Swedes, Norwegians, Danes, and Icelanders are all closely related, and so are the languages they speak. The Finns speak a very different language, as do the Saami or Lapps, a people who live in the far north.

The region is rich in natural resources such as timber, iron ore, and offshore oil and gas from the North Sea. The Icelandic economy depends on catching and processing fish. Iceland also uses energy from its volcanic rocks to heat greenhouses for garden produce. Sweden, Denmark, and Finland are members of the European Union.

Fish are dried on the Norwegian coast. The Scandinavian countries are almost surrounded by sea. Fishing is a major industry, and Scandinavian cooking includes many recipes for herring or cod.

Danish pastries are delicious, sweet rolls and twists, which are often iced and filled with raisins or other fruit. They are eaten mid-morning, with cups of strong coffee.

In winter the Swedish countryside is covered in snow and temperatures drop below zero. Summers are warm but brief. This landscape lies near Uddevalla in the southwest, which enjoys a milder climate than the east of the country.

The towers and gables of Egeskov Castle are reflected in the still waters of the lake. This fortress was built in 1554 on the island of Fyn in southern Denmark. At that time Denmark and Norway were still united, but Sweden had already broken away from the union. These were troubled times in Danish history. Today the castle serves as a tourist attraction and includes a transportation museum.

Isafjördur

Vatneyri

Hólmavík

Bordeyri

Húsavik

Saudárkrókur

Akureyri

Seydisfjördur

ICELAND

Vatnajökull

Akranes

REYKJAVIK

Keflavík

▲ Oraefajökull
6,952 ft.

Vestmannaeyjar

Finland

Denmark

Iceland

Norway

Sweden

NORTH ATLANTIC OCEAN

ARCTIC OCEAN

Hammerfest

Vadsø

Kirkenes

0 50 100 150 200 250 Kilometers

0 50 100 150 Miles

Tromsø

Mt. Haltia 4,344 ft.

Lapland

Narvik

Svolvær

Kebnekaise 6,926 ft.

Sodankylä

Kiruna

N

Bodø

Rovaniemi

Övertorneå

Kemi

Mosjøen

Luleå

Storuman

Skellefte

Skellefteå

Oulu

Kuopio

RUSSIA

SWEDEN

Umeå

Kokkola

Joensuu

Kristiansund

Trondheim

Östersund

Vaasa

Ume

Jyväskylä

Ålesund

Galdhøpiggen 8,100 ft.

Sundsvall

Kaskö

FINLAND

NORWAY

Särna

Tampere

Lillehammer

Gulf of Bothnia

Lahti

Bergen

Västerdal

Turku HELSINKI

Gávle

Uppsala

Åland Is.

Gulf of Finland

OSLO

Karlstad

STOCKHOLM

ESTONIA

Stavanger

Skien

Örebro

Lake Vänern

Kristiansand

Baltic Sea

Linköping

Göteborg

Borås

Västervik

Gotland

Skagerrak

Kattegat

Borgholm

Aalborg

DENMARK

Århus

Karlskrona

COPENHAGEN

Kristianstad

Esbjerg

Odense

Malmö

GERMANY

Lapps in traditional costume gather outside a stave church in northern Norway, a part of the country known as Lapland. Many of these wooden churches date from the time of the Vikings.

Netherlands, Belgium &

Netherlands means "lowlands" and much of this country lies below the level of the North Sea. Over the ages Dutch engineers became experts at flood control and at reclaiming land from the sea. The flat Dutch farmland is crossed by canals and rivers. The Dutch were also great seafarers and during the 1600s their overseas trade brought wealth to cities such as Amsterdam. Today the Netherlands is famous for its electrical and chemical industries, dairy products, vegetables, and flowers. Rotterdam is the world's largest seaport.

Neighboring Belgium is mostly flat, but to the south the land rises to the hills of the Ardennes. Belgium is heavily industrialized, producing steel, chemicals, and electronics. Its textile industry dates back to the Middle Ages. Tiny Luxembourg, set amidst rolling farmland and woods, is one of the wealthiest nations in Europe, being a world center of banking.

All three countries have strong historical and economic ties and together helped to set up the European Economic Community (today's European Union) in the 1950s. The region is home to Frisians, Dutch, the closely related Flemings of Belgium, Walloons (French-speaking Belgians), Luxemburgers (who speak a dialect called Letzebuergesch), people of Asian and African descent, and other European nationals.

The Netherlands are often referred to as "Holland," which is really just the name of the region.

A Belgian worker makes fine chocolates by hand. Belgium is famous throughout Europe for excellent chocolate, delicious Ardennes pâtés and meats, fried potatoes, and strong beers. Home-grown food crops include wheat, barley, oats, rye, potatoes, and sugar beet. However, the Belgian economy today depends more on its efficient factories and businesses than on its traditional farming produce.

The pond bat is found in this part of Europe, although it is becoming increasingly scarce. It likes to live on marshy lowlands. It hunts by night, swooping over ponds and ditches in search of water insects.

The Atomium monument in Brussels was built for the 1958 World's Fair as a modern symbol of science and progress. Brussels today is not only the capital of Belgium but is also the headquarters of many European Union institutions, such as the European Parliament, Commission, and Monetary System, in addition to NATO.

Luxembourg City rises above the Alzette River. It is an important center of business and is the seat of the European Court of Justice. It has the palace of the Grand Dukes and a fine cathedral.

Large, round Dutch cheeses are laid out at Alkmaar near Amsterdam in the Netherlands. Mild Dutch cheeses such as Edam and Gouda are an important export. The Dutch themselves prefer the stronger tasting farmhouse cheeses.

In spring tourists come from around the world to see the windmills and the fields of brightly colored tulips. Bulbs and seeds for flowers is an important business. The windmills were originally built for controlling the water level.

Luxembourg

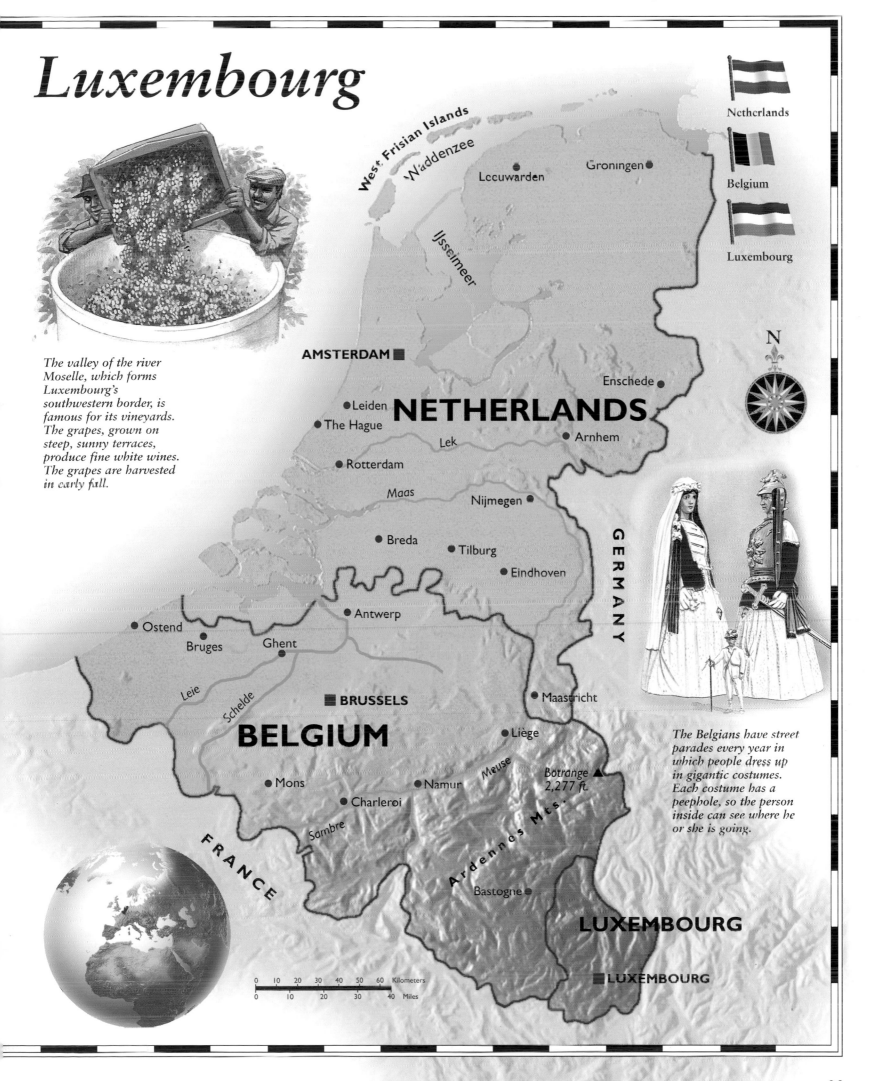

The valley of the river Moselle, which forms Luxembourg's southwestern border, is famous for its vineyards. The grapes, grown on steep, sunny terraces, produce fine white wines. The grapes are harvested in early fall.

Netherlands

Belgium

Luxembourg

West Frisian Islands

Waddenzee

Leeuwarden

Groningen

IJsselmeer

N

AMSTERDAM

Enschede

Leiden

NETHERLANDS

The Hague

Lek

Arnhem

Rotterdam

Maas

Nijmegen

Breda

Tilburg

G
E
R
M
A
N
Y

Eindhoven

Antwerp

Ostend

Bruges

Ghent

Maastricht

Leie

Schelde

■ BRUSSELS

Liège

BELGIUM

Mons

Namur

Meuse

Botrange ▲ 2,277 ft.

Charleroi

Sambre

The Belgians have street parades every year in which people dress up in gigantic costumes. Each costume has a peephole, so the person inside can see where he or she is going.

F
R
A
N
C
E

Ardennes Mts.

Bastogne

LUXEMBOURG

■ LUXEMBOURG

| 0 | 10 | 20 | 30 | 40 | 50 | 60 | Kilometers |
| 0 | 10 | 20 | 30 | 40 | Miles |

The British Isles

The British Isles lie in shallow waters off the coast of northwestern Europe. They are bordered to the west by the Atlantic Ocean. The climate is mild and western shores receive a heavy rainfall, making the fields green.

There are about 5,000 islands, many of them very small. The two largest ones are Great Britain and Ireland. Great Britain is made up of three countries called England, Scotland, and Wales, which together form the United Kingdom. The northern part of Ireland is governed by the United Kingdom, but most of Ireland forms a separate, independent republic. Both the United Kingdom and the Irish Republic are members of the European Union. The Isle of Man and the Channel Islands have self-government, but still have close ties with the United Kingdom. Peoples of the British Isles include English, Irish, Scots, Welsh, Jews, Roma (Gypsies), Asians, and Afro-Caribbeans.

The British Isles include areas of rich farmland for growing crops and for raising cattle and sheep. The world's first big factories were built here in the 1800s, when Britain was the center of a worldwide empire. There are still many big cities. More people now work providing services such as banking than in heavy industries.

The hardy Highland cattle, with their long shaggy coats, were bred for the harsh climate of the Scottish mountains. The Highland region, a stronghold of ancient Gaelic traditions and language, lives by farming, fishing, forestry, and tourism.

Tenby, known in the Welsh language as Dinbych y Pysgod, is in southern Wales. The beautiful western shores of the British Isles are always popular with vacationers.

Horses are sold at this fair in the town of Drimoleague in the Irish Republic. The Irish countryside is famous for breeding horses for the farm and the racetrack.

Irish stew is one of the best known Irish dishes. It is made of mutton, onions, potatoes, leeks, and carrots, and is served with dumplings.

Saint Paul's is one of the finest cathedrals in England. Lying at the heart of London, it was rebuilt between 1675 and 1710 by an architect called Christopher Wren.

The barrier above, to the east of London, is designed to prevent the Thames River flooding the capital city during North Sea gales. Completed in 1984, its concrete piers support ten steel gates. Normally the gates lie on the river bottom. When tides rise above normal levels, the gates revolve upward.

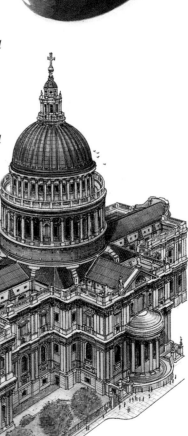

United Kingdom

Ireland

Orkney Is. • Kirkwall

• Thurso

• Stornoway

Outer Hebrides

Slye

Loch Ness • Inverness • Peterhead

SCOTLAND • Aberdeen

Grampian Highlands

▲ Ben Nevis 4,406 ft.

Mallaig •

Tay

Oban • Perth • • Dundee

ATLANTIC OCEAN

North Sea

N

Glasgow •

■ **Edinburgh**

Clyde

Ayr • *Tweed*

Southern Uplands

Lerwick

Shetland Is.

• Londonderry • Newcastle

Tyne

Stranraer • Carlisle • Durham

NORTHERN IRELAND ■ **Belfast**

Lake District • Middlesbrough

Pennines

Sligo • • Armagh

Swale

IRELAND

• Dundalk

Isle of Man

Blackpool • • Leeds • Kingston-upon-Hull

Irish Sea **Bradford**

Manchester •

Athlone • Liverpool • • Sheffield

Galway • Liffey ■ **DUBLIN**

ENGLAND

Shannon Wrexham • • Nottingham

• Carlow Derby •

Limerick • **Cambrian Mts.** *Trent* • Peterborough • Norwich

Tipperary • Wolverhampton •

Birmingham • • Coventry • Cambridge

Waterford • Aberystwyth • *Severn* • Northampton • Ipswich

Carrauntoohill ▲ • Killarney *Wye* • Luton

3,414 ft **WALES** Carmarthen • • Gloucester • Colchester

Cork • Swansea • Oxford • **LONDON** • Canterbury

Bantry • **Cardiff** • Bristol *Thames* • Dover

Reading •

ATLANTIC OCEAN **Exmoor** Salisbury • Folkestone

Southampton • • Portsmouth • Brighton

Bournemouth •

Dartmoor • Exeter

Land's End • Plymouth

English Channel

• Penzance

0 50 100 150 Kilometers
0 50 100 Miles

CHANNEL ISLANDS

35

France

France   Monaco

France is a republic that lies at the heart of western Europe. It stretches from the English Channel in the north to the warm Mediterranean Sea in the south. Western borders are formed by the Atlantic Ocean and by the high peaks of the Pyrenees. To the east rise the Alps and the Jura and Vosges mountains. The French countryside includes plains, the rugged highlands of the Massif Central, and beautiful river valleys.

The wide range of climates makes it possible to grow a variety of crops, including wheat, corn, peaches, apples, and grapes. French vineyards produce many of the world's finest wines. France is also a major industrial power, specializing in building cars, trains, and aircraft. French fashions and perfumes are famous around the world. France is a leading member of the European Union, which it helped to found. Monaco, a tiny independent nation in the southeast, keeps very close links with its much larger neighbor.

French cooking, or cuisine, is said to be the best in the world and is much admired. Quiche Lorraine is a pastry tart filled with beaten eggs, cheese, cream, chopped bacon, and herbs. Lorraine is in the northeast of the country. Each region of France has its own special dishes.

In Paris a shining modern pyramid stands side-by-side with the Louvre, a 16th-century palace that now houses one of the world's great art collections. France has been a center of the arts for more than a thousand years.

Pine logs are stacked at a mill in the region of Bordeaux. France has large areas of commercially managed forest in the southwest, as well as in the Massif Central and the east.

France is a land of ancient castles, or châteaux, but these soaring towers are fakes, just a few years old. Disney, the American entertainments corporation, designed this fairytale theme park outside Paris. It is visited by children from all over Europe.

The iron structure of the Eiffel Tower, 984 feet high, is the most famous landmark in Paris, the French capital. It was built for a great exhibition held in 1889 to mark the 100th anniversary of the French Revolution. Paris, one of Europe's finest cities, has a total population of more than eight million. Built on the banks of and islands of the Seine River, it is a center of government and business.

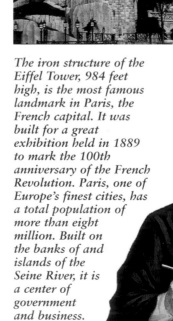

The Provence region is bordered by Italy, the Mediterranean coast, and the Rhône Valley. It enjoys mild winters and hot summers. Lavender, grapes, mulberries, olives, and citrus fruits grow in its peaceful countryside.

This elderly lacemaker wears the traditional costume of her district in Brittany. The Breton people have their own language, culture, and traditions, as do the Catalans and Basques of the southwest and the Corsicans of the Mediterranean. Other citizens are descended from peoples of France's former overseas empire.

0 50 100 150 Kilometers
0 50 100 Miles

N

Dunkerque
Calais
Boulogne
Lille
Arras
BELGIUM

English Channel

Charleville-Mézières
LUXEMBOURG

GERMANY

Cherbourg
Le Havre
Dieppe
Amiens
Reims
Metz

Rouen
Marne
Châlons-sur-Marne
Strasbourg
Nancy
Vosges Mountains

Caen
Seine
PARIS

St.-Malo
Chartres
FRANCE
Colmar
Mulhouse

Brest
St.-Brieuc
Fontainebleau
Seine
Troyes
Rhine

Quimper
Rennes
Moselle

Lorient
Le Mans
Orléans
Saône
Dijon
Besançon
Doubs

Loire

Angers
Tours
Loire

St. Nazaire
Nantes
Cher
Bourges
Jura Mountains

SWITZERLAND

Poitiers
Mâcon
Saône

La Rochelle
Montluçon

Clermont-Ferrand
Lyon
Loire
Rhône

Cognac
Limoges
St-Etienne
Mt.Blanc 15,771 ft.

Mt. Dore 6,188 ft.

Massif Central
Grenoble
Isère
Drac
Alps

Bordeaux
Dordogne
Cère
Valence

ITALY

Bay of Biscay
Lot
Durance

Garonne
Lot
Aveyron
Rhône
Verdon

Avignon
Durance
MONACO

Montauban
Tarn
Nîmes
Aix-en-Provence
Nice

Biarritz
Adour
Toulouse
Montpellier
Cannes

Bayonne
Garonne
Carcassonne
Béziers
Marseille

Pau
Ariège
Aude
Toulon

Lourdes
Pyrenees
Perpignan
Mediterranean Sea

SPAIN
ANDORRA

Bastia

**CORSICA
(France)**

Ajaccio

Bonifacio

Germany

In southern Germany there are evergreen forests and the snowy peaks of the Alps, while in the north there are rolling hills, heath lands, and coastal sand dunes. The Rhine River winds through sunny vineyards in the west. Around the rivers Oder and Neisse, along the eastern border, stretch the plains of central Europe. Here the climate is warm in summer but very cold in winter.

In the Middle Ages, Germany was divided into hundreds of small states and cities. The country was united in 1871, but was divided again (into two parts, the Federal Republic of Germany in the west and the German Democratic Republic in the east) between 1945 and 1990, after Germany's defeat in World War II.

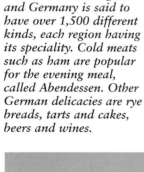

Germany today is a Federal Republic, with many laws being made at a regional level. The country is divided into 16 states called *Länder*. Each region has its own spoken dialects of German, style of architecture, customs, and traditions. Germany has many large cities. The capital, in the northeast of the country, is Berlin.

Germany is a member of the European Union and is an important center of industry and trade. The country is famous for its car manufacturing and its chemical and electronic industries. Factories employ many workers from other parts of Europe, such as Turkey. The eastern part of Germany, which was organized on communist lines before 1990, is going through many industrial changes. Germany has an important tourist industry. Its attractions include medieval castles and winter sports.

Wurst means sausage, and Germany is said to have over 1,500 different kinds, each region having its speciality. Cold meats such as ham are popular for the evening meal, called Abendessen. Other German delicacies are rye breads, tarts and cakes, beers and wines.

Modern office blocks tower above traditional buildings in the city of Frankfurt-am-Main. Frankfurt is the home of the German stock exchange and is a centre of banking and insurance. Many international trade fairs are held in the city.

The Kiel Canal is the busiest shipping canal in the world, being used by more than 40,000 ships a year. At 61 miles long, it provides a vital link between the North Sea and the Baltic Sea. Germany's northern coast includes major European ports such as Bremen, Hamburg, Lübeck, and Rostock.

A tractor harvests sugar beet on the north German plain. Many farms in the south are small and family owned. Farms in the east have always been much larger.

Germany

DENMARK

Baltic Sea

North Sea

● Flensburg

● Kiel

● Stralsund

● Neumünster

● Rostock

● Lübeck

● Schwerin

Bremerhaven

● Wilhelmshaven

● Hamburg

● Bremen

● Lüneburg

Weser

Elbe

Oder

POLAND

NETHERLANDS

● Celle

Aller

■ **BERLIN**

Ems

● Hannover

● Brunswick

● Brandenburg

Frankfurt an
der Oder

● Bielefeld

Weser

Leine

● Hildesheim

Harz Mts.

● Magdeburg

Neisse

● Münster

Elster

● Cottbus

Rhine

● Paderborn

● Dessau

● Essen

● Dortmund

● Kassel

● Halle

● Leipzig

● Duisburg

Elbe

● Düsseldorf

● Wuppertal

● Mühlhausen

● Dresden

● Cologne

● Erfurt

● Chemnitz

● Aachen

● Marburg

● Gera

● Bonn

Zwickau

Ore Mountains

● Geissen

GERMANY

● Plauen

BELGIUM

● Koblenz

Main

CZECH REPUBLIC

Eifel

● Wiesbaden

Mosel

Rhine

● Frankfurt-am-Main

● Bayreuth

LUXEMBOURG

● Mainz

● Darmstadt

● Bamberg

● Trier

● Würzburg

Bohemian Forest

● Mannheim

● Nuremberg

● Heidelberg

● Regensburg

FRANCE

● Heilbronn

● Karlsruhe

Danube

● Ingolstadt

● Stuttgart

● Passau

N

Swabian Jura

● Augsburg

Rhine

● Ulm

**Black
Forest**

● Freiburg

● Munich

**Lake
Constance**

▲ Zugspitze
2,721 ft.

SWITZERLAND

A l p s

AUSTRIA

Switzerland and its neighbors

Switzerland is famous for its dairy herds, which produce cheeses such as Emmenthaler and Gruyère. These may be melted in a pot, mixed with white wine, and seasoned to make a fondue. Pieces of bread are dipped into the delicious mixture on special forks.

The snowy mountain ranges of the Alps form a massive barrier between northern and southern Europe. Some of the highest peaks are in Germany, France, and Italy, but many lie within the borders of three Alpine nations—Switzerland, Liechtenstein, and Austria. The ice and rock of the summits give way to green Alpine pastures, filled with wildflowers in summer. These drop steeply toward forested valleys and deep lakes. Melting snows from the Alps are the source of Western Europe's greatest rivers, including the Rhine, the Rhône, the Po, and the Inn-Danube river system.

Communications and transportation through the Alps have always been very hazardous. Routes to the south now pass through deep tunnels bored through the rock. The Simplon, between Switzerland and Italy, is the world's longest rail tunnel, opened in 1922. It is 12.3 miles long. The St. Gotthard Road tunnel of 1980, at 10.2 miles, holds the world record for any motor vehicle tunnel.

Switzerland is a small country divided into districts called cantons. Four languages may be heard, namely French, German, Italian, and Romansh. Although Switzerland has few natural resources apart from hydroelectric power, it has become a wealthy country through the manufacture of clocks, watches, and precision instruments. It is a center of banking and tourism. The spectacular mountain scenery, with its lakes, waterfalls, and pretty villages, attracts winter sports enthusiasts and summer vacationers. Switzerland is neutral, having kept out of European wars since 1815. Its capital, Geneva, is the headquarters of many bodies such as the International Red Cross and the World Health Organization.

Liechtenstein, to the east, is a tiny German-speaking state which has managed to avoid being swallowed up by its more powerful neighbors. It is ruled by a prince, but laws are passed by an elected government. Closely linked with Switzerland, it uses the Swiss franc as its currency.

Balzers lies on slopes rising from the valley of the Rhine River, in the extreme south of Liechtenstein. Tourists visit this little Alpine principality in search of mountain scenery and snow for winter skiing.

The Matterhorn rises to 14,692 feet above sea level. This dramatic peak is in the Swiss canton of Valais, near the Italian border. It was in the Alps that mountain climbing first became popular, and many climbers come here each year.

Switzerland has many colorful festivals. In spring and fall, herds of goats or cows decorated with flowers and bells are led to and from their summer pastures high in the mountains. In winter, too, people celebrate saints' days and carnivals.

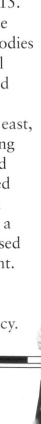

The white-tailed eagle is a powerful, dark-brown bird of prey with a white, wedge-shaped tail. It is a rare sight soaring over Austrian lakes in winter months. Its main breeding grounds lie to the east, in the Balkans and eastern Europe. Like many European birds of prey, it has suffered from being overhunted.

Austria

A small country today, Austria once ruled a vast Central European empire. The country is a German-speaking republic, and its capital, Vienna, has many grand historical buildings.

Much of the country is made up of forested mountain slopes, whose timber is used for paper making, for building the broad-roofed chalets of the Alps, and for wood carving. Many tourists visit the ski slopes in winter. The east of the country descends to flat lands around the Danube River and this is where most industry and agriculture is based. Austria has few natural resources but exports textiles, chemicals, electrical goods, and machinery. It is a member of the European Union and its major trading partner is Germany.

Switzerland

Liechtenstein

Austria

N

0   50   100   150   200 Kilometers
0   50   100   150 Miles

CZECH REPUBLIC

FRANCE   LIECHTENSTEIN   GERMANY   Linz   Danube

Basel   Salzburg   VIENNA

Zurich   AUSTRIA

BERN   Innsbruck   ▲ Grossglockner

Swiss Alps   12,457 ft.   Central Alps   Graz

Geneva   HUNGARY

SWITZERLAND   ▲ Dufourspitze   ITALY

15,203 ft.   SLOVENIA

Vienna's Burgtheater was built in the 1800s. As capital of the old Austro-Hungarian empire, Vienna was a center of architecture, opera, popular drama, music, dance, and the visual arts. One of the most famous Viennese composers was Johann Strauss the Younger (1835–1899), whose popular waltz tunes, such as "The Blue Danube", became a lasting symbol of the city.

Cut glass is produced at Rattenberg, in the Lower Inn valley of the Tirol. The Alpine lands have enjoyed a long tradition in hand crafts such as wood carving, toy making, leather work, weaving, felt making, and the delicate decoration of fine porcelain.

Spain and Portugal

Beyond the high mountain ranges of the Pyrenees, the Iberian peninsula juts out from southern Europe between the Atlantic Ocean and the Mediterranean Sea. The land is mostly mountainous, with a broad central plateau. The northwest is green, kept moist by Atlantic rains, but much of the country bakes under the summer sun. It is hot and dusty, and parts are in danger of becoming desert. The region includes many beautiful cities, with palaces and cathedrals dating from the early Middle Ages, when Muslims from North Africa ruled the region, and Christian knights fought against them. The Iberian peninsula produces cork, olives, corn, sunflowers, oranges, and grapes for wine, sherry, and port. Cattle are bred in many areas, and bullfighting is an ancient tradition. Large fishing fleets are based around the coast and the blue seas, and sunny beaches attract many tourists. Engineering, chemical and textile production, and food processing are major industries.

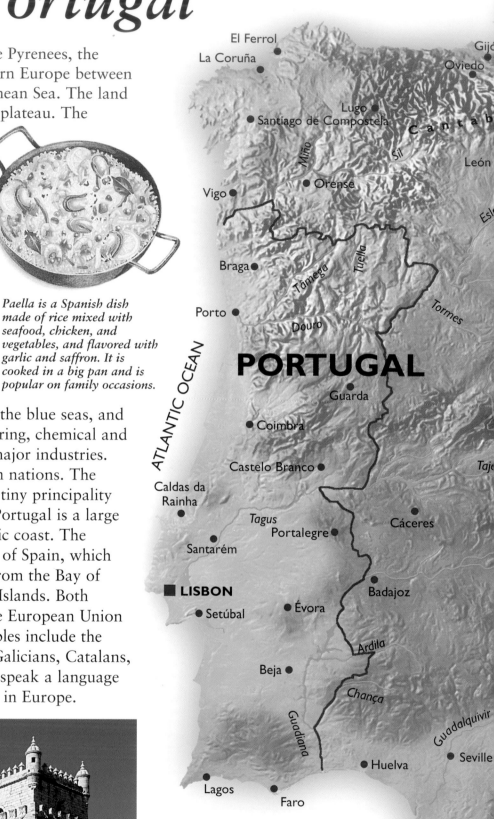

Paella is a Spanish dish made of rice mixed with seafood, chicken, and vegetables, and flavored with garlic and saffron. It is cooked in a big pan and is popular on family occasions.

There are three Iberian nations. The smallest is Andorra, a tiny principality high in the Pyrenees. Portugal is a large republic on the Atlantic coast. The largest is the kingdom of Spain, which stretches all the way from the Bay of Biscay to the Balearic Islands. Both Spain and Portugal are European Union members. Iberian peoples include the Portuguese, Spanish, Galicians, Catalans, and the Basques, who speak a language unrelated to any other in Europe.

The Algarve is an area of southern Portugal that has a beautiful coastline. It is very popular with tourists and is a center for fishing.

The Torre de Belem was built in Lisbon harbor in 1520 to protect ships sailing to and from Lisbon, the Portuguese capital. At this time Portugal was starting to build up a large overseas empire.

Spain is one of the world's largest exporters of citrus fruits. These include sweet mandarins, lemons, and oranges from Seville.

Spain

Portugal

Andorra

Bay of Biscay

Santander

San Sebastián

FRANCE

Bilbao

an Mountains

Vitoria

Pamplona

Pyrenees

ANDORRA

Andorra la Vella

Figueras

Burgos

Logroño

Ebro

Arga

Gállego

Llobregat

Gerona

Manresa

Tarrasa

Valladolid

Duero

Soria

Ebro

Cinca

Lérida

Barcelona

SPAIN

Jalón

Saragossa

Reus

Caspe

Tarragona

Tortosa

Avila

Guadalajara

Tajuna

Tajo

Alcalá de Henares

Teruel

Morella

Vinaroz

N

MADRID

Mijares

MENORCA

Toledo

Aranjuez

Cuenca

Castellón de la Plana

MALLORCA

Mahón

Turia

Palma

Manacor

Valencia

Villarroblédo

Júcar

IBIZA

Guadiana

Albacete

Ibiza

Ciudad Real

Alcoy

Mediterranean Sea

Puertollano

Segura

Alicante

Linares

Murcia

Córdoba

Jaén

Lorca

Cartagena

Genil

Aguilas

Granada

Sierra Nevada

Every town in Spain has its own fairs, or fiestas. Many of these mark religious festivals, while others commemorate historical events. At Toledo, near Madrid, parades may include figures wearing the masks of giants, devils, clowns and animals.

Almería

Málaga

Motril

Marbella

BRALTAR (U.K.)

0   50   100   150 Kilometers

0   25   50   75 Miles

43

Italy and its neighbors

Spaghetti served with a Bolognese sauce of meat and tomato is just one of the many pasta dishes that have made Italian cooking popular around the world.

Italy is a long, boot-shaped peninsula, stretching southward into the Mediterranean Sea. The country also includes two large islands, Sicily and Sardinia. The northern mainland takes in the lakes and towering mountains of the Alps and the fertile plains around the Po River. The Apennine Mountains form a rugged backbone down the center of the country, and in the south there are active volcanoes.

The climate of Italy is warm enough for farmers to grow olives, citrus fruits, and grapes. Fishing fleets catch tuna and sardines. Many people work in tourism; others work in factories, producing cars, clothes, leather goods, and computers. Most industry is based in the wealthier north. Italy was a founding member of the European Union. In ancient times Rome ruled most of western Europe, but Italy was later divided into many small states until it was reunited in 1861. On the peninsula, there are still two tiny independent states. Vatican City is the headquarters of the Roman Catholic Church, and San Marino is a republic in the Apennines. Malta is another independent country, with its own language and way of life. These tiny islands lie between Sicily and North Africa. Malta's economy depends on its naval dockyards and on tourism.

Vineyards cover the sunny hillsides of Chianti, in the central region of Tuscany. The grapes produce a strong red wine. Grapes have been grown in Italy for thousands of years. Today it is the biggest wine producer in the world.

Venice is a fine city built on mud islands on the northern Adriatic coast. It is famous for its canals, bridges, and gondolas, which are traditional black boats guided by poles.

St. Peter's Square lies within Vatican City, the area of Rome that comes under the rule of the Roman Catholic Church. Many Christians come here to be blessed by the Pope, or to visit the great basilica of St. Peter's. The Vatican City, or "Holy See", is the world's smallest independent country, covering just 0.17 square miles. Its population is about 10,000.

Many tourists come to see the Leaning Tower, in the ancient university town of Pisa. Work on the beautiful marble tower began over 800 years ago, but it was built on sinking ground and soon began to tilt over at an angle. It leans over by 16 feet from the vertical.

In Sardinian and Spanish costumes, horsemen take to the streets in Oristano on the island of Sardinia during the Sartiglia Festival, which has celebrated the start of spring since medieval times. The Sards speak their own dialect of Italian and have kept up many ancient traditions. Over the centuries, many different civilizations have invaded Sardinia, each bringing its customs.

0   50   100   150 Kilometers
0   25   50   75   100 Miles

SWITZERLAND

AUSTRIA

Bolzano

▲ Mt. Ortles
12,812 ft.

SLOVENIA

Mt. Blanc
15,771 ft.

Bergamo

Udine

FRANCE

A l p s

Ticino

Milan

Brescia

Verona

Piave

Trieste

Turin

Oglio

Padua

Venice

Tanaro

Po

CROATIA

Mt. Viso
12,602 ft.

Parma

Ferrara

Reno

Modena

Genoa

Bologna

Ravenna

MONACO

La Spezia

Rimini

San Marino

SAN MARINO

Ancona

Adriatic Sea

Florence

A
p
e
n

Pisa

Arno

Ligurian Sea

Livorno

Perugia

Bastia

Elba

CORSICA
(France)

Terni

Tiber

Pescara

Ajaccio

n
i
n
e
s

ROME

VATICAN
CITY

ITALY

Foggia

Bonifacio

Ofanto

Bari

Sassari

Naples

Potenza

Brindisi

Mt. Vesuvius ▲
4,000 ft.

Salerno

Taranto

Tirso

Senise

Oristano

Tyrrhenian Sea

SARDINIA
(Italy)

Cagliari

Cosenza

Catanzaro

Lipari
Islands

*Revelers wear masks and cloaks
for the carnival in Venice. For
hundreds of years, Venice was
the most important center for
trade between Europe and the
East, and so became very rich.*

Palermo

Messina

Reggio di Calabria

Trapani

SICILY
(Italy)

▲ Mt. Etna
10,900 ft.

Agrigento

Catania

Mediterranean Sea

Syracuse

N

MALTA

Valletta

Italy

San Marino

Vatican City

Malta

45

Central Europe

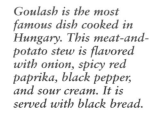

Warsaw, the Polish capital since 1550, lies on the Vistula River. Much of it was rebuilt after bitter fighting during the Second World War (1939–1945). Today, Warsaw has a population of more than 1,655,000 and is a center of business, industry, such as car manufacture, and communications.

A great plain covers the northern part of Poland. Sunny in the summer but bitterly cold and snowy in winter, it is drained by the Bug and Vistula rivers. To the south, the land rises to the Tatra Mountains. Polish farmers grow potatoes, flax, rye, and beets. Poland has large forests and reserves of coal, sulphur, silver, and mineral salt. In some areas the land has been badly polluted by industry.

In 1993 Czechoslovakia, to the south, split into two separate countries, the Czech Republic and the Slovak Republic. These regions include high mountains and forests, wooded hills and fertile farmland. The Czechs produce paper, glass, steel, and the original Pilsener beer. The Slovaks mine iron ore, raise pigs, and grow cereal crops.

Across the winding Danube River are the plains and rolling hills of Hungary, where vineyards produce strong red wines and orchards supply fruit for preserving and jam making.

Central Europe is home to Slavic peoples such as the Poles, Czechs, and Slovaks, to the Magyars of Hungary, and to Roma (Gypsies), Germans, and Jews. In the Middle Ages there were powerful kingdoms in Central Europe, and many beautiful cities date from then. The region later came under the rule of more powerful neighbors such as Turkey, Austria, Russia, and Germany. From 1947 until 1990 the whole of Central Europe was ruled by communist governments.

Goulash is the most famous dish cooked in Hungary. This meat-and-potato stew is flavored with onion, spicy red paprika, black pepper, and sour cream. It is served with black bread.

Hungary's Houses of Parliament stand on the Danube River in the capital, Budapest. There are 88 statues outside the building.

Prague, capital and largest city of the Czech Republic, rises from the banks of the Vltava River (below). In the Middle Ages it was capital of a kingdom called Bohemia and was a center of learning and the arts. Prague, although now industrialized, is still a beautiful old city which has recently become one of the most popular destinations for tourists in Europe.

The jangling sound of the zither is common in Central European folk music. The zither is a flat, many-stringed instrument which is plucked with a thumb-pick or strummed with the fingertips.

Slovaks, a Slavic people, make up the majority of the population of Slovakia. This Orthodox church is a fine example of Slavic folk architecture. It is built in a traditional design, with stepped roofs and onion domes.

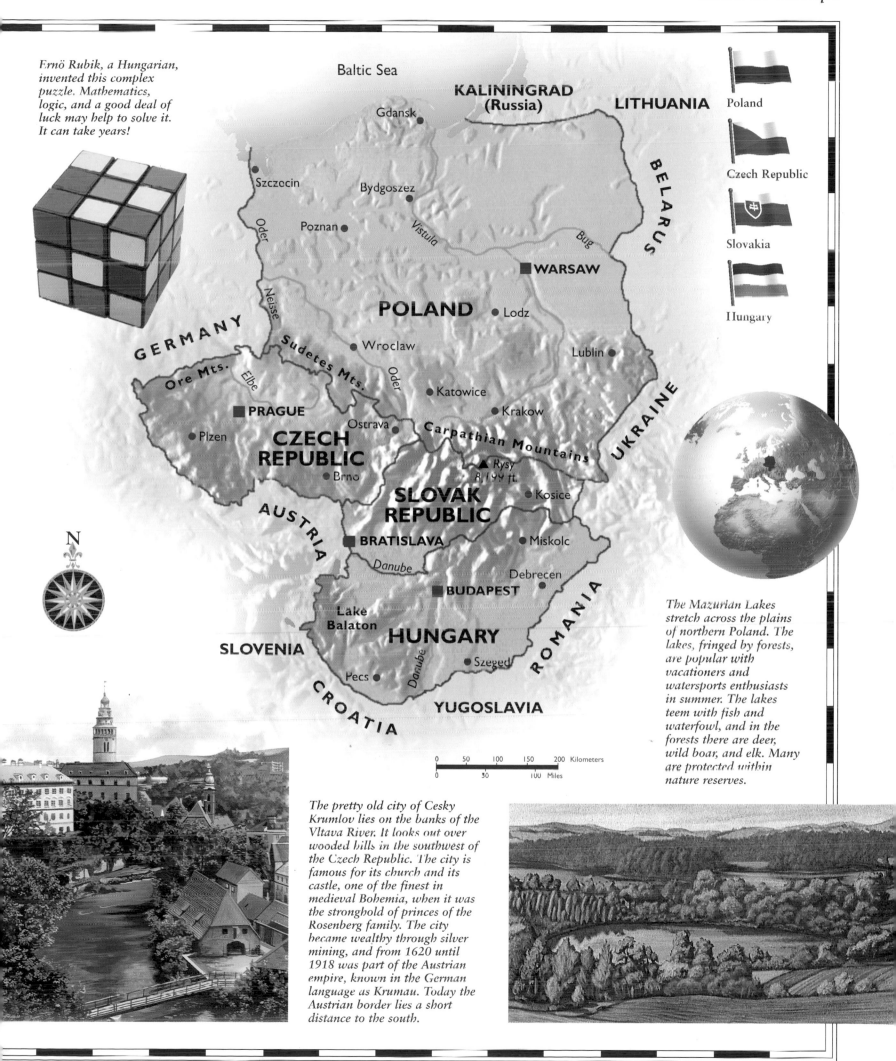

Ernö Rubik, a Hungarian, invented this complex puzzle. Mathematics, logic, and a good deal of luck may help to solve it. It can take years!

Baltic Sea

KALININGRAD (Russia)

LITHUANIA

Gdansk

Szczecin

Bydgoszez

Poznan

Oder

Vistula

Bug

BELARUS

■ **WARSAW**

POLAND

Lodz

Wroclaw

Lublin

GERMANY

Neisse

Sudetes Mts.

Oder

Ore Mts.

Elbe

Katowice

UKRAINE

■ **PRAGUE**

Ostrava

Krakow

Plzen

CZECH REPUBLIC

Brno

Carpathian Mountains

▲ Rysy 8199 ft.

Kosice

SLOVAK REPUBLIC

AUSTRIA

■ **BRATISLAVA**

Miskolc

Danube

■ **BUDAPEST**

Debrecen

ROMANIA

SLOVENIA

Lake Balaton

HUNGARY

Danube

Szeged

Pecs

CROATIA

YUGOSLAVIA

N

Poland

Czech Republic

Slovakia

Hungary

0   50   100   150   200 Kilometers
0   30   100 Miles

The Mazurian Lakes stretch across the plains of northern Poland. The lakes, fringed by forests, are popular with vacationers and watersports enthusiasts in summer. The lakes teem with fish and waterfowl, and in the forests there are deer, wild boar, and elk. Many are protected within nature reserves.

The pretty old city of Cesky Krumlov lies on the banks of the Vltava River. It looks out over wooded hills in the southwest of the Czech Republic. The city is famous for its church and its castle, one of the finest in medieval Bohemia, when it was the stronghold of princes of the Rosenberg family. The city became wealthy through silver mining, and from 1620 until 1918 was part of the Austrian empire, known in the German language as Krumau. Today the Austrian border lies a short distance to the south.

The Balkan states

T he Balkan peninsula is a broad mass of land that extends southward from central Europe into the eastern Mediterranean. Its coastline borders the Adriatic, Black Sea, and the Mediterranean. Much of the region is rugged and mountainous, with areas of fertile plains. Winters can be bitterly cold in the north and summers can be very hot and dry, especially in the south.

The region is home to many peoples. There are Slavic peoples, such as Slovaks, Slovenians, Croats, Serbs, and Bosnian Muslims, as well as Roma (Gypsies), Magyars (Hungarians), Romanians, Bulgars, Turks, Albanians, and Greeks. Between 1990 and 1991 the former republic of Yugoslavia broke up into five different nations—Slovenia, Croatia, Bosnia-Herzegovina, Yugoslavia (Serbia-Montenegro), and the Former Yugoslav Republic of Macedonia. Disputes over the new borders led to terrible wars in the early 1990s. Albania and Romania have also suffered unrest in recent years.

The Balkan peninsula becomes narrower to the south of Bulgaria, and breaks up into ragged headlands and island chains. Here is Greece, a land of brown rocks, blue seas, whitewashed villages, ancient ruins, and medieval churches. Cities such as Athens are full of wonderful reminders of the ancient Greek civilizations that greatly influenced the European way of life.

Farmers in the Balkans produce corn, sunflowers, melons, grapes for wine, fruit, olives, and tobacco. Greece has been a member of the European Union since 1981 and every year attracts tourists from all over the world.

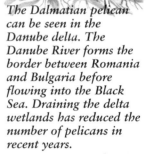

In 1989 there was an uprising in Romania, which had a form of communist government. There were strikes, riots, and fighting in the capital, Bucharest. The unpopular ruler, President Nicolae Ceausescu, was overthrown and shot.

The Dalmatian pelican can be seen in the Danube delta. The Danube River forms the border between Romania and Bulgaria before flowing into the Black Sea. Draining the delta wetlands has reduced the number of pelicans in recent years.

The Corinth Canal, over 3.7 miles long, was opened in 1893. It offers a direct route for shipping from the Gulf of Corinth to Piraeus, the port of Athens. This narrow strip of water separates the large peninsula of the Peloponnesus from the central mainland.

This amphitheater at Pula in Croatia was built by the Romans in A.D. 80. The whole of the Balkan peninsula was once part of the Roman Empire.

Greek food is popular in many parts of the world. This salad is made from tomatoes, cucumber, black olives, and cubes of feta, a white goat's cheese. The dressing of olive oil is mopped up with crusty white bread.

The first Olympic Games were held in Olympia in 776 B.C. This statue of a discus thrower was made by the Greek sculptor Myron around 450 B.C.

N

0 100 200 300 Kilometers
0 50 100 150 200 Miles

UKRAINE

MOLDOVA

AUSTRIA

HUNGARY

SLOVENIA
Ljubljana

Carpathians

ROMANIA

Zagreb

CROATIA

Transylvanian Alps

BOSNIA-
HERZEGOVINA

Belgrade

Bucharest

Sarajevo

Danube

YUGOSLAVIA

BULGARIA

Black
Sea

Adriatic Sea

Sofia

Skopje

MACEDONIA

Tirane

ALBANIA

GREECE

TURKEY

Thessaloniki

Aegean Sea

Pindus Mts.

Athens

Peloponnesus

Kalamai

Rhodes

Khania   Iráklion
Crete

Albania

Romania

Bulgaria

Slovenia

Croatia

Greece

Macedonia

Yugoslavia

Bosnia-
Herzegovina

Apples are sorted and packed into crates at this factory in Peshkepi, in eastern Albania. Albanian crops include grapes, wheat, corn, potatoes, and beets, but this small, mountainous country has little fertile farmland and the summers are hot and dusty.

The Iron Gates are part of the spectacular gorge of Samaria on the island of Crete. This large Mediterranean island is a part of Greece. Many tourists visit its beautiful mountains and coastline and its ancient ruins, some of which date back more than 4,000 years.

The medieval Church of St. John at Caneo, by Lake Ohrid in the Former Yugoslav Republic of Macedonia. Greece has disputed the right of this new country to use the name Macedonia, the same name as the ancient Greek kingdom in the north of Greece.

Russia and its neighbors

Armenia

Kyrgyzstan

The Russian Federation is the world's biggest country, stretching from the Gulf of Finland to the Pacific Ocean. Its northern coastline borders the Arctic Ocean, and most of the land suffers from severe winters. The west of the country lies in Europe, while the lands to the east of the Ural Mountains lie in Asia. The deep-frozen tundra of the far north gives way to a belt of coniferous forest called taiga. In the southwest is the rich black earth of the steppes, grasslands used mainly to grow cereals. The neighboring lands to the south include deserts and high mountains. The whole region is rich in natural resources including oil, natural gas, minerals, and timber.

From the 1500s onward Russia built up a vast empire under the rule of emperors called tsars. In 1917 communist revolutionaries seized power and killed the tsar. The new state, which became known as the Soviet Union, set about becoming one of the world's great industrial powers. It underwent political reforms in the 1980s and abandoned communism in 1990. During this period many of the countries which had been part of the Soviet Union broke away to become independent nations—the Baltic states of Latvia, Lithuania, and Estonia, the eastern European states of Ukraine and Belarus, and the borderlands of the far south. Russia itself remains home to many different ethnic groups.

This church at Ananuri, in Georgia, was built in 1689. Fortified walls were raised to protect it from attack by Turkish and Persian armies.

St. Basil's Cathedral is in Moscow's Red Square. Many Russian Orthodox churches have beautiful, onion-shaped domes.

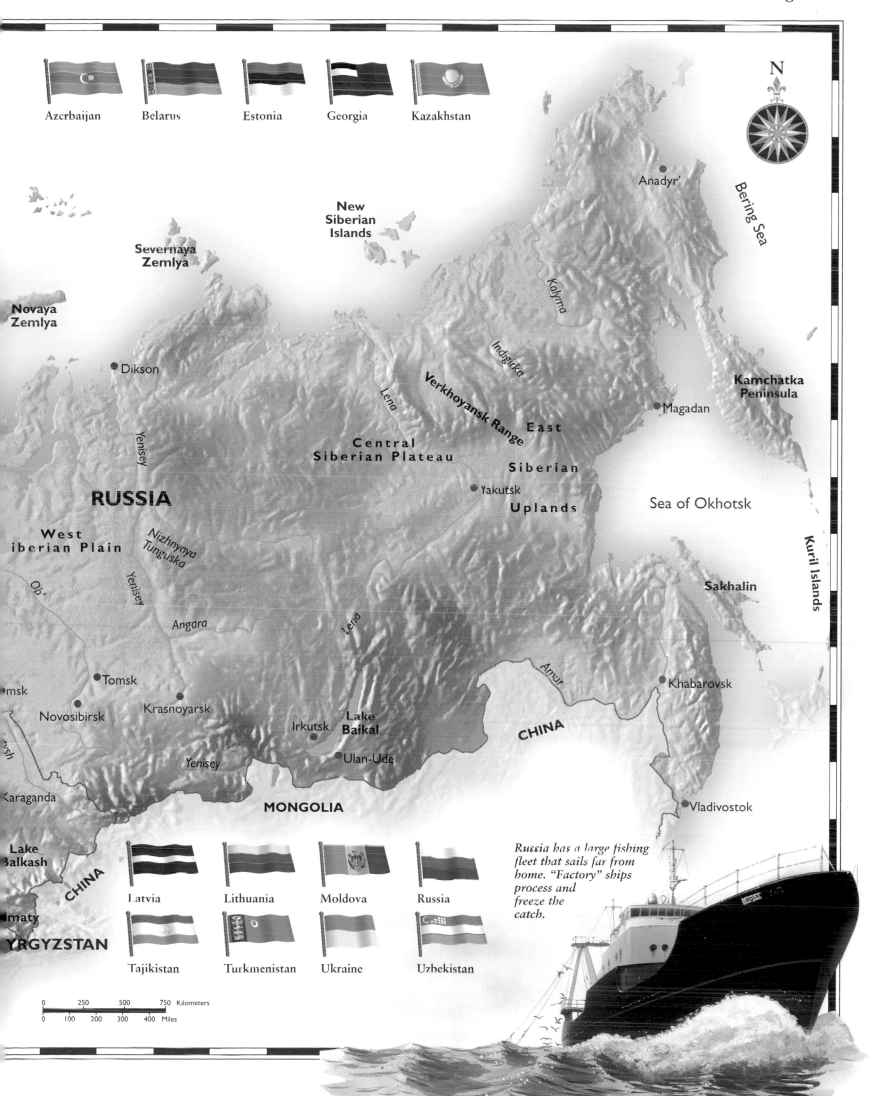

N

Azerbaijan Belarus Estonia Georgia Kazakhstan

Bering Sea

Anadyr'

New
Siberian
Islands

Severnaya
Zemlya

Kolyma

Novaya
Zemlya

Indigirka

Kamchatka
Peninsula

Dikson

Verkhoyansk Range

Lena

East

Central
Siberian Plateau

Yenisey

Magadan

RUSSIA

Siberian

Yakutsk

Sea of Okhotsk

Uplands

West
iberian Plain

Nizhnyaya
Tunguska

Kuril Islands

Ob'

Yenisey

Sakhalin

Angara

Lena

Tomsk

Amur

Khabarovsk

msk

Krasnoyarsk

Novosibirsk

Irkutsk

Lake
Baikal

CHINA

Yenisey

Ulan-Ude

Vladivostok

Karaganda

MONGOLIA

Lake
Balkash

*Russia has a large fishing
fleet that sails far from
home. "Factory" ships
process and
freeze the
catch.*

CHINA

maty

Latvia Lithuania Moldova Russia

YRGYZSTAN

Tajikistan Turkmenistan Ukraine Uzbekistan

| 0 | 250 | 500 | 750 | Kilometers |
| 0 | 100 | 200 | 300 | 400 | Miles |

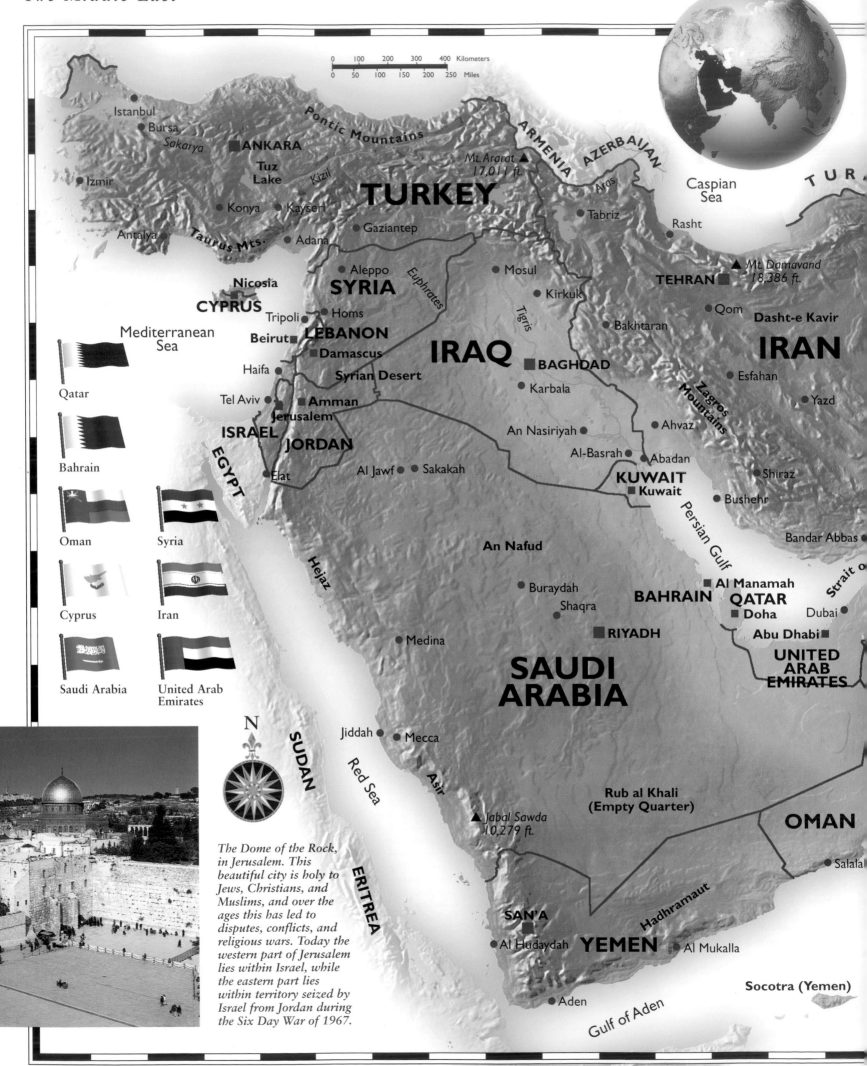

0 100 200 300 400 Kilometers
0 50 100 150 200 250 Miles

Istanbul
Bursa
Sakarya
ANKARA
Izmir
Tuz Lake
Konya
Kizil
Kayseri
Antalya
Taurus Mts.
Adana

Pontic Mountains

ARMENIA
AZERBAIJAN

Mt. Ararat ▲
17,011 ft.
Aras

Caspian Sea

TUR

TURKEY

Gaziantep

Tabriz
Rasht

Aleppo
Euphrates
Mosul
Kirkuk
▲ Mt. Damavand
18,386 ft.
TEHRAN

SYRIA
Homs
Qom

Nicosia
CYPRUS
Tripoli
LEBANON
Beirut
■ **Damascus**
Haifa
Syrian Desert

Tigris
Bakhtaran

Dasht-e Kavir

IRAQ
■ **BAGHDAD**
Karbala

IRAN

Esfahan
Yazd

Mediterranean Sea

Tel Aviv
■ **Amman**
Jerusalem
ISRAEL
JORDAN

An Nasiriyah
Ahvaz

Al-Basrah
Abadan

Zagros Mountains

Shiraz

EGYPT
Elat
Al Jawf
Sakakah

KUWAIT
■ **Kuwait**

Bushehr

Bandar Abbas

An Nafud

Persian Gulf

Strait o

Hejaz

Buraydah
Shaqra

BAHRAIN
■ **Al Manamah**
QATAR
■ **Doha**
Dubai

Medina

■ **RIYADH**

Abu Dhabi ■

UNITED ARAB EMIRATES

SAUDI ARABIA

N

Jiddah
Mecca

Red Sea

Asir

Rub al Khali
(Empty Quarter)

OMAN

SUDAN

▲ Jabal Sawda
10,279 ft.

Salala

ERITREA

SAN'A
■
Al Hudaydah

Hadramaut

Al Mukalla

YEMEN

Aden
Gulf of Aden

Socotra (Yemen)

Qatar

Bahrain

Oman

Syria

Cyprus

Iran

Saudi Arabia

United Arab Emirates

The Dome of the Rock, in Jerusalem. This beautiful city is holy to Jews, Christians, and Muslims, and over the ages this has led to disputes, conflicts, and religious wars. Today the western part of Jerusalem lies within Israel, while the eastern part lies within territory seized by Israel from Jordan during the Six Day War of 1967.

The Middle East

Iraq

Turkey

Israel

Jordan

The Middle East is bordered to the north by mountains, by the rolling grasslands or steppes of eastern Europe and by the Caspian and Black Sea coasts. To the west is the Mediterranean Sea and to the south the warm waters of the Red Sea, Persian Gulf, and Indian Ocean. There are fertile lands in the north and west and along the rivers Tigris and Euphrates. However, much of the area, including the vast Arabian peninsula, is taken up by harsh, empty desert.

This part of Asia is sometimes called the Near East or Southwest Asia. It was here that humans first began to farm and build towns, more than 12,000 years ago. Three of the world's most widespread religions—Judaism, Christianity, and Islam—grew up here.

The Middle East is populated by Greeks, Jews, Arabs, Turks, Kurds, and Iranians. There are many political and religious conflicts in the region, threatening peace in Cyprus, Israel, Turkey, Iraq, Iran, and Kuwait. The most important resource is oil, which has brought great wealth to the families who rule the Arab states around the Gulf. Supertankers carry oil from these deserts to ports all over the world.

Petra is a ruined city in Jordan, in which the buildings are carved out of the cliffs. The city once lay on important trading routes and was capital of the Nabatean kingdom until A.D. 106, when it was conquered by the ancient Romans.

The Madrasa-i Chahar Bagh (right), in the Iranian city of Isfahan, has been a center of religious study since the 1700s. Iran is a strictly Islamic country where religious leaders have a major say in government.

Yemen

Kuwait

Lebanon

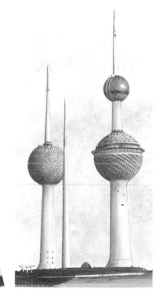

These unusual looking towers are part of a desalination scheme in Kuwait. This useful but expensive process takes the salt out of seawater to make it drinkable. Supplying enough water for drinking and irrigation is a major problem in the desert states around the Gulf.

In the Cappadocia region of Turkey, near Konya, strange rock formations tower above the plains. Homes have been carved out of the rocks and built on to them, making them look like beehives.

Quinces stuffed with minced lamb and flavored with cinnamon make up an Iranian dish that has been cooked since the days of the ancient Persians. Iranian meals may be served with black tea and large, flat, freshly baked nan breads.

This massive castle in Syria (below) is called Krak des Chevaliers. It dates back to 1205. In the Middle Ages, Christian and Muslim armies fought for control of Palestine or "Holy Land," in wars called Crusades.

India and its neighbors

The Himalaya mountain range, which includes many of the world's highest peaks, separates the great mass of land known as the Indian subcontinent from central Asia and China. Melting snows feed great rivers such as the Ganges which spill across the plains of northern India. The mountainous nations of the north are sparsely populated, while the lands to the south—Pakistan, Bangladesh, India, and Myanmar (Burma)—are very crowded. The island nation of Sri Lanka lies in the Indian Ocean, across the Palk Strait.

The subcontinent extends south to the tropics, where it is extremely hot, with winds and torrential rains during the monsoon season.

India and the neighboring lands make up a melting pot of many different peoples, cultures, and languages. These have shaped some of history's greatest civilizations, and the region is the birthplace of many religions, including Hinduism, Buddhism, Sikhism, and Jainism. Afghanistan, Pakistan, and Bangladesh are Muslim countries, and there are also many Muslims within the borders of India.

The region often suffers from earthquakes, drought, and flooding, and poverty is widespread. Crops include wheat, rice, coconuts, sugar-cane, tea, and cotton. Factories produce textiles, vehicles, steel, fertilizers, and computer software. India has a large film industry based in the city of Bombay.

Htamin le thoke is a dish eaten in Myanmar (Burma). It includes all sorts of snacks made from leftovers —noodles, rice, spinach, and onions. It is served with tamarind sauce. Tamarind seeds and pulp come from the pod of a tropical tree.

Kashmir is a beautiful region of high valleys, snowy peaks, and lakes. It stretches across the Himalaya range on the borders of India, Pakistan, and China. Most Kashmiris are Muslims, and some of them have fought a campaign to break away from the Indian state.

Kathakali is a form of traditional dancing to be seen in southern India. The dancers, with painted faces and dressed in traditional costumes, retell ancient stories about the Hindu gods and demons.

Elephants and dancers parade through the streets of Kandy, in Sri Lanka, in a great procession, or "perahera". It is held each summer to honor a holy relic of the Buddha.

The Ganges River forms a maze of waterways before it reaches the Bay of Bengal. Many of the villages on its banks and islands are at risk from flooding during the monsoon rains.

This street market is in Goa, on India's west coast near Hubli-Dharwar. Indian markets are crowded with traders, people haggling over prices, fortune-tellers, and showmen. All kinds of food, clothes, tools, pots, and pans are on sale. Markets in Goa might specialize in selling coconuts, tropical fruits such as bananas, rice, and delicious fresh fish caught locally in the Indian Ocean.

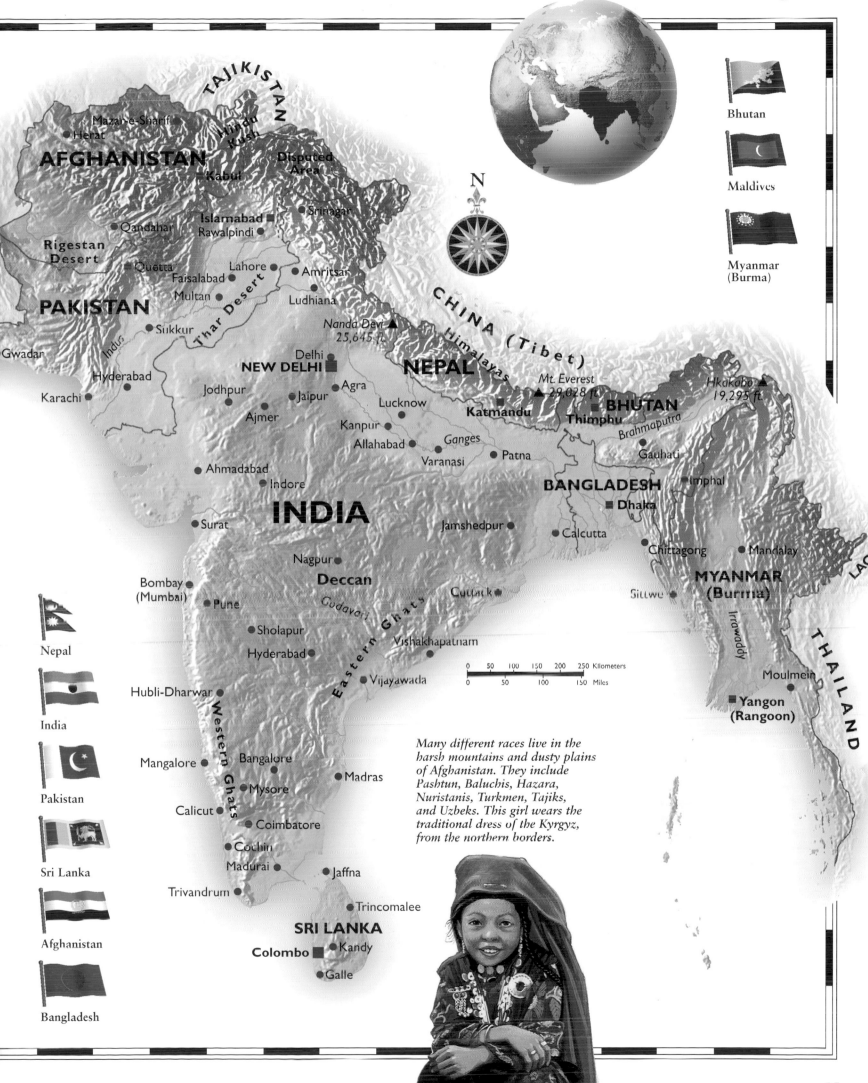

Bhutan

Maldives

Myanmar (Burma)

N

TAJIKISTAN

Mazar-e-Sharif
Herat

Hindu Kush

AFGHANISTAN

Kabul

Disputed Area

Srinagar

Qandahar

Islamabad
Rawalpindi

Rigestan Desert

Quetta

Lahore
Faisalabad

Amritsar

PAKISTAN

Multan

Ludhiana

Gwadar

Sukkur

Indus

Thar Desert

Nanda Devi ▲
25,645 ft.

CHINA (Tibet)

Hyderabad

Delhi

NEW DELHI

Himalayas

NEPAL

Mt. Everest
▲ 29,028 ft.

Hkakabo ▲
19,295 ft.

Karachi

Jodhpur

Agra

Jaipur

Lucknow

Katmandu

BHUTAN
Thimphu

Ajmer

Kanpur

Brahmaputra

Allahabad

Ganges

Gauhati

Varanasi

Patna

Imphal

Ahmadabad

Indore

BANGLADESH

Dhaka

INDIA

Surat

Jamshedpur

Calcutta

Chittagong

Mandalay

Nagpur

Deccan

Cuttack

MYANMAR (Burma)

Bombay (Mumbai)

Pune

Godavari

Sittwe

Hyderabad

Sholapur

Eastern Ghats

Vishakhapatnam

Irrawaddy

THAILAND

Vijayawada

Moulmein

Hubli-Dharwar

Mangalore

Bangalore

Western Ghats

Madras

■ **Yangon (Rangoon)**

Mysore

Calicut

Coimbatore

Cochin

Madurai

Jaffna

Trivandrum

Trincomalee

SRI LANKA

Colombo ■
Kandy

Galle

LAOS

50 100 150 200 250 Kilometers
0 50 100 150 Miles

Nepal

India

Pakistan

Sri Lanka

Afghanistan

Bangladesh

Many different races live in the harsh mountains and dusty plains of Afghanistan. They include Pashtun, Baluchis, Hazara, Nuristanis, Turkmen, Tajiks, and Uzbeks. This girl wears the traditional dress of the Kyrgyz, from the northern borders.

China and its neighbors

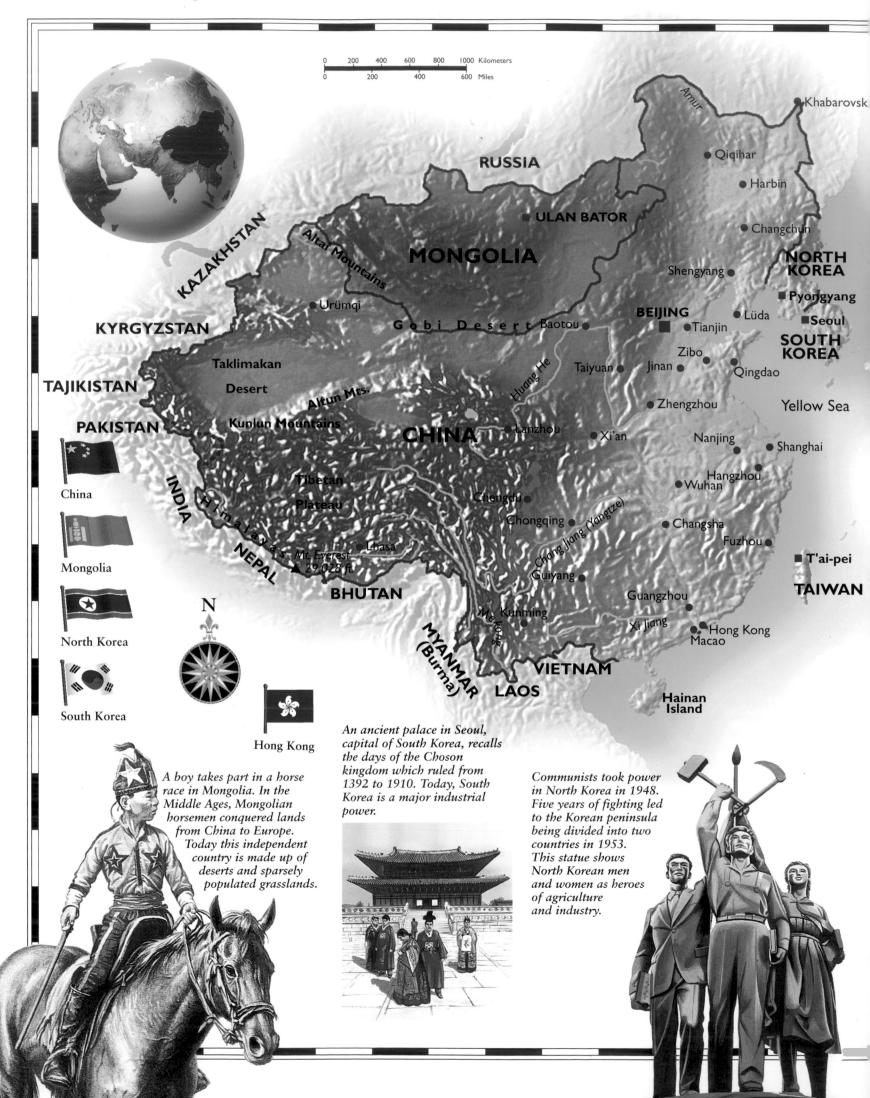

RUSSIA

Khabarovsk

Amur

Qiqihar

Harbin

Changchun

ULAN BATOR

MONGOLIA

Shengyang

NORTH KOREA

KAZAKHSTAN

Altai Mountains

Gobi Desert

Baotou

BEIJING

Tianjin

Lüda

Pyongyang

Seoul

Urümqi

KYRGYZSTAN

SOUTH KOREA

TAJIKISTAN

Taklimakan Desert

Altun Mts.

Huang He

Taiyuan

Jinan

Zibo

Zhengzhou

Qingdao

Yellow Sea

PAKISTAN

Kunlun Mountains

CHINA

Lanzhou

Xi'an

Nanjing

Shanghai

China

INDIA

Tibetan Plateau

Chengdu

Chongqing

Hangzhou

Wuhan

Changsha

Fuzhou

Mongolia

Himalayas

NEPAL

Mt. Everest 29,028 ft

Lhasa

Chang Jiang (Yangtze)

Guiyang

North Korea

BHUTAN

Mekong

Kunming

Guangzhou

Xi Jiang

T'ai-pei

TAIWAN

South Korea

MYANMAR (Burma)

LAOS

VIETNAM

Hong Kong

Macao

Hainan Island

Hong Kong

An ancient palace in Seoul, capital of South Korea, recalls the days of the Choson kingdom which ruled from 1392 to 1910. Today, South Korea is a major industrial power.

A boy takes part in a horse race in Mongolia. In the Middle Ages, Mongolian horsemen conquered lands from China to Europe. Today this independent country is made up of deserts and sparsely populated grasslands.

Communists took power in North Korea in 1948. Five years of fighting led to the Korean peninsula being divided into two countries in 1953. This statue shows North Korean men and women as heroes of agriculture and industry.

China and its neighbors

More people live in China than in any other country in the world. This vast country is ringed by remote deserts and towering mountain ranges. Great rivers rise in the mountains and flow across the crowded, fertile plains of the south and east. The coastline borders the Yellow Sea and the East and South China seas. Northern regions have bitterly cold winters, while the south is warm and humid.

Many different peoples live in China, including Tibetans, Uygurs, Mongols, and Zhuang. Nine out of ten Chinese belong to the Han ethnic group. China has one of the world's most ancient civilizations and for thousands of years it was ruled by powerful emperors. In 1949 the Chinese Communist Party seized power. It is still in power today, but its economic polices have changed a great deal in recent years. China grows tea, rice, corn, and wheat. Industries include textiles, oil, steel, engineering, electronics, and household goods.

In 1949 Chinese people who opposed communism set up their own government on the island of Taiwan. The British colony of Hong Kong returns to Chinese rule in 1997, and the Portuguese colony of Macao in 1999. China's neighbors include Mongolia to the north and North and South Korea to the east.

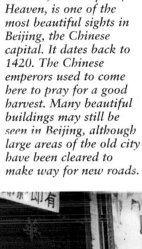

Chow mein is a southern Chinese dish made up of noodles, shredded chicken or meat, and stir-fried vegetables. Chinese people who have settled in other lands have made their food popular all around the world.

Tiantan, the Temple of Heaven, is one of the most beautiful sights in Beijing, the Chinese capital. It dates back to 1420. The Chinese emperors used to come here to pray for a good harvest. Many beautiful buildings may still be seen in Beijing, although large areas of the old city have been cleared to make way for new roads.

Water buffalo cross the Li Jiang at Yangshuo, near Guilin. In the background are limestone rock formations, a favorite subject for Chinese artists over the ages. Many tourists visit this beautiful region of southern China. While many Chinese cities are huge industrial centers, wide areas of the countryside remain peaceful and unspoiled.

In the Middle Kingdom theme park in Hong Kong costumed stilt walkers celebrate the Chinese Spring Festival (New Year) in traditional style. Each new year is named after a different animal.

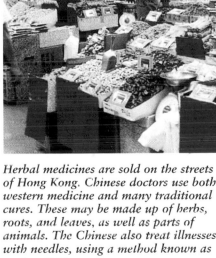

Herbal medicines are sold on the streets of Hong Kong. Chinese doctors use both western medicine and many traditional cures. These may be made up of herbs, roots, and leaves, as well as parts of animals. The Chinese also treat illnesses with needles, using a method known as acupuncture.

Japan

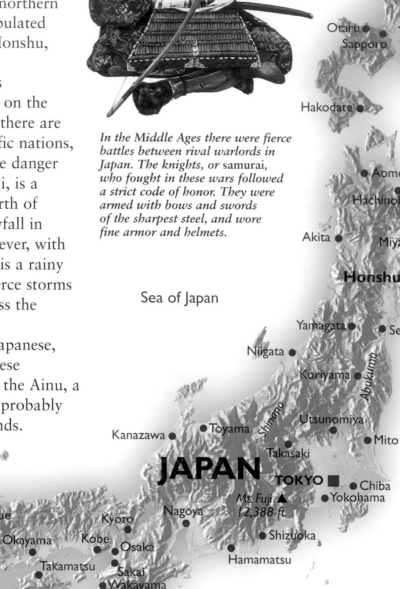

Japan is a country made up of islands. There are about 3,000 of them in all, forming a long chain down the Pacific coast of northern Asia. The largest and most populated islands are called Hokkaido, Honshu, Shikoku, and Kyushu.

Because much of the land is mountainous, most people live on the crowded coastal plains, where there are very big cities. Like many Pacific nations, Japan lies within an earthquake danger zone. Its highest mountain, Fuji, is a volcano. The climate in the north of Japan is cool, with heavy snowfall in winter. The south is mild, however, with warm, humid summers. There is a rainy season in June and July and fierce storms called typhoons may rage across the coasts in September.

Most of the population is Japanese, but there are Korean and Chinese minorities. In the far north are the Ainu, a pale-skinned people who were probably the first inhabitants of the islands. Many Japanese have settled in other parts of the world, such as the United States.

In the Middle Ages there were fierce battles between rival warlords in Japan. The knights, or samurai, who fought in these wars followed a strict code of honor. They were armed with bows and swords of the sharpest steel, and wore fine armor and helmets.

Soya Point

Asahigawa • **Hokkaido**

Otaru • Ishikari
Sapporo • Kushiro •

Hakodate •

N

Aomori •
Hachinohe •

Sea of Japan

Akita • Miyako •

Honshu

Yamagata • Sendai •
Niigata •
Koriyama •

Abukuma

Kanazawa • Toyama • Utsunomiya •
Shinano Mito •
Takasaki •
JAPAN TOKYO ■ Chiba •
Mt. Fuji ▲ Yokohama •
12,388 ft.

Matsue •
Kyoro • Nagoya • Shizuoka •
Okayama • Kobe •
Hiroshima • Osaka • Hamamatsu •
Takamatsu •
Sakai •
Wakayama •

Kitakyushu •
Fukuoka • Matsuyama • Tokushima •

Kochi •
Oita • **Shikoku**
Nagasaki • NORTH PACIFIC
Kumamoto • OCEAN

Kyushu

Miyazaki •
Kagoshima •

Japan

Kyoto, the former capital of Japan, has many beautiful wooden temples, shrines, and gardens. Buddhism came to Japan from China in A.D. 552, and many of its beliefs merged with those of the native Shinto religion. Many Japanese respect both Buddhist and Shinto traditions.

| 0 | 50 | 100 | 150 | 200 Kilometers |
| 0 | 50 | 100 | | 150 Miles |

Land of the Rising Sun

In the Japanese language, Japan is called "Nippon," which means "Source of the Sun." The national flag shows a red sunrise. Respect for tradition and the forces of nature survive in the Japanese religion called Shinto.

Japan is said to have been ruled by emperors since 660 B.C. Its ancient civilization, influenced by that of China, produced the finest pottery, silk textiles, architecture, and paintings. The same skills may be seen in modern industrial design.

In the 1930s and 1940s Japan attacked and invaded many other Asian countries, before being defeated by the Allies in 1945. Two Japanese cities were destroyed by terrible atomic bombs. Japan recovered rapidly, however. Although it had few natural resources, it became one of the world's greatest economic powers, producing electronic goods and cars. Finance and banking have become major industries.

Japan makes the most of the small amount of good farmland it does have. Its chief crop is rice, and it also grows tea, fruit, soybeans, wheat, barley, and sweet potatoes. Japanese fishing fleets find a ready market for their catches back home, where fish forms a big part of their diet.

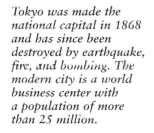

Tokyo was made the national capital in 1868 and has since been destroyed by earthquake, fire, and bombing. The modern city is a world business center with a population of more than 25 million.

Fuji, a sacred mountain in Japanese tradition, is one of the most beautiful mountains in the world. Its volcanic slopes, topped with snow, have been a favorite subject for Japanese artists through the ages.

Sushi is a treat for the eye as well as the tastebuds. Beautifully prepared and displayed snacks of raw fish, vegetables, seaweed, and shrimp are served with small mounds of rice.

Buyo *means "dance" in Japanese, and traditional Japanese dancers train for many years. The movements are centuries old and are accompanied by a* shamisen, *a three-stringed instrument.*

Sumo wrestling is a popular sport in Japan. The heavyweight wrestlers aim to make their opponent's body touch the ground. The action is usually over within seconds. However, the wrestlers spend long hours preparing for the contest with special exercises and rituals.

Southeast Asia

The part of Asia extending eastward from India and southward from China is sometimes called Indo-China. This region takes in Myanmar (Burma), Thailand, Laos, Cambodia, and Vietnam. Jungle-covered hills slope down to fertile plains crossed by great rivers such as the Irrawaddy and the Mekong. The climate is hot and humid with seasonal heavy, monsoon rains.

A long, thin peninsula stretches southward to Malaysia and the small city-state of Singapore. Malaysia, Indonesia, Brunei, and the Philippines occupy the long chains of islands that stretch eastward into the Pacific Ocean.

The region is home to a great variety of peoples, cultures, religions, and languages. Southeast Asia was torn apart by war from the 1940s until the 1970s. The regional economy depends on rice and fruit farming, forestry, rubber, and palm oil. Natural resources include oil and natural gas. Tourism, already a major industry in Thailand and Bali, is growing in countries such as Vietnam. Big cities such as Singapore and Jakarta are centers of international business and finance.

Rice has been farmed on these flooded terraces, on the Philippine island of Luzon, for more than 2,000 years. In recent years new, improved strains of rice have been developed at research stations in the Philippines.

Bangkok, the capital of Thailand, has hundreds of beautiful Buddhist temples. Buddhism plays a big part in the lives of the Thai people, many of whom become monks who wear orange robes and shave their heads.

The Indonesian island of Bali is famous for its beautiful religious festivals and its court and temple dances. The Balinese follow the Hindu faith, whereas most Indonesians are Muslims.

Vietnamese women wash a crop of carrots in the Mekong River. The vegetables are placed in big wicker baskets. The women protect their heads from the hot sun with the large straw hats that are popular in the lands around the South China Sea.

Buddha Park, outside the Laotian capital of Vientiane, contains many large religious statues. The park was set aside in the 1950s in order to honor both the Buddhist and Hindu faiths.

Satay is a popular dish in Malaysia and other Southeast Asian countries. Small pieces of meat or chicken are placed on a wooden skewer and barbecued, before being served with a hot peanut sauce.

N

Brunei Laos Malaysia Thailand Vietnam Indonesia

Cambodia

Philippines

Singapore

CHINA

MYANMAR (Burma)

Red

Hanoi ■ Haiphong

Chiang Mai

LAOS

Vientiane

THAILAND

Da Nang

Mekong

Bangkok

CAMBODIA VIETNAM

Phnom Penh ● Nha Trang

Ho Chi Minh City

Gulf of Thailand

South China Sea

Luzon PACIFIC OCEAN

● Manila

PHILIPPINES

Cebu

Sulu Sea

Mindanao ● Davao

Zamboanga

Ipoh

MALAYSIA

Medan

Kuala Lumpur

Bandar Seri Begawan

BRUNEI

EASTERN MALAYSIA

B o r n e o

Celebes Sea

SINGAPORE

Batanghari

Pontianak Kapuas

Padang

Sumatra

Jambi

Balikpapan

Sulawesi (Celebes)

Palembang

Barito

Banjarmasin

Java Sea

Ujung Pandang

Jakarta

I N D O N E S I A

Bandung Java Surabaya

Malang Bali Flores Timor

Timor Sea

These children have dressed up in fancy costumes in order to celebrate Brunei's Independence Day. Brunei's population includes both Malays and Chinese. This small nation on the coast of Borneo gained full independence from Great Britain in 1984.

0 100 200 300 400 500 Kilometers

0 100 200 300 Miles

61

North Africa

The Sahara is one of the hottest places on Earth, a shimmering wilderness of sand, rock, and gravel which stretches across the continent. The Atlas Mountains run along the desert's northwestern fringes, descending to the fertile Mediterranean coast of the "Maghreb" lands—Algeria, Morocco, and Tunisia. The "Sahel" lands, those to the south of the Sahara, have sparse, dusty grassland and suffer from droughts, when many people go hungry.

Egypt too is a land of deserts, but the Nile River brings valuable water to its farmland. Thanks to this, Egypt became the center of an ancient civilization whose splendid temples and tombs may still be seen today. Branches of the Nile also flow through Sudan, Africa's largest country, and through the mountainous lands of Ethiopia.

North Africa is home to the Berbers and to the Arabs, who conquered the region in the A.D. 600s. In the south there are many different Black African peoples, such as the Nuer, Dinka, and Shilluk of Sudan, the Amhara of Ethiopia, and the Hausa, Fulani, and Kanuri of the Sahel. Most of the region is Muslim, but there are Christians in Egypt, Ethiopia, and southern Sudan.

A Berber water-seller offers passersby a cool drink from his goatskin sack. Many Berbers live in the Atlas Mountains and on the fringes of the Sahara desert. Some are farmers, while others are nomadic herders and traders.

A mysterious statue, known as the Sphinx, guards the ancient royal tombs of the pyramids. The pyramids stand on the edge of the desert at Giza, near the modern Egyptian capital of Cairo. The ancient Egyptian civilization thrived from about 3100 until 1085 B.C. Its rulers were called pharaohs.

Beg wot is a thick stew made in Ethiopia. It is cooked with meat, tomatoes, and hot peppers. Here, it is served with basil leaves and eggplant on a doughy bread called injera. Ethiopian farmers raise cattle and crops, but food is often scarce.

Goat skins are dyed in big vats in Morocco, particularly in Fez and Marrakesh. The smell from these vats is horrible, because pigeon droppings are used during the dyeing process. The country is famous for its fine crafts, particularly soft leather, woolen rugs, brass, and copper. Many of these are bought by tourists in the markets, or souks.

A piper plays a traditional instrument at a festival at Ghadamis, in Libya. Arabic music and dialects of the Arabic language are still heard throughout the countries of the North African coast, as they have been since the seventh century.

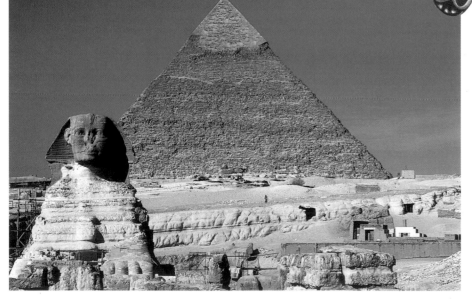

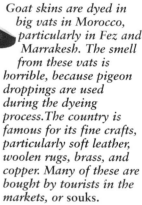

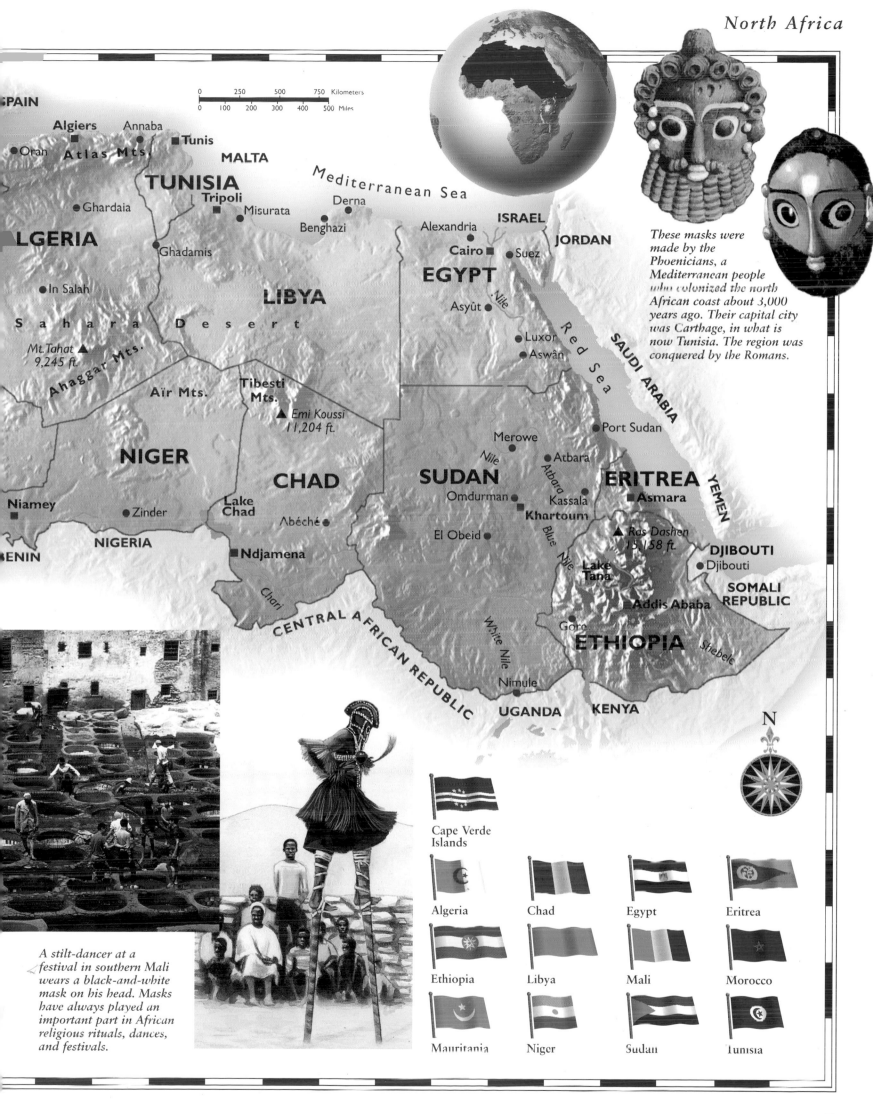

SPAIN

Algiers   Annaba

Oran   **Atlas Mts.**   ■ Tunis

TUNISIA   **MALTA**

ALGERIA   • Ghardaia   ■ **Tripoli**   • Misurata   • Derna

• Ghadamis   • Benghazi   Alexandria   **ISRAEL**

JORDAN

Cairo ■   • Suez

• In Salah   **EGYPT**

LIBYA   Asyût •   *Nile*

S a h a r a   D e s e r t   • Luxor

Mt. Tahat ▲   **Ahaggar Mts.**   • Aswân   *Red Sea*   **SAUDI ARABIA**

9,245 ft.

Air Mts.   **Tibesti Mts.**

▲ Emi Koussi   11,204 ft.   **YEMEN**

NIGER   Merowe •   • Port Sudan

Nile   • Atbara

CHAD   **SUDAN**   *Atbara*   **ERITREA**

Niamey ■   • Zinder   **Lake Chad**   Omdurman •   Kassala •   ■ **Asmara**

• Abéché   **Khartoum**   ▲ Ras Dashen   15,158 ft.

NIGERIA   El Obeid •   *Blue Nile*   *Lake Tana*   **DJIBOUTI**

BENIN   ■ **Ndjamena**   • Djibouti

Chari   **SOMALI REPUBLIC**

Addis Ababa ■

CENTRAL AFRICAN REPUBLIC   *White Nile*   Gore •   **ETHIOPIA**   *Shebele*

Nimule •

UGANDA   **KENYA**   **N**

These masks were made by the Phoenicians, a Mediterranean people who colonized the north African coast about 3,000 years ago. Their capital city was Carthage, in what is now Tunisia. The region was conquered by the Romans.

A stilt-dancer at a festival in southern Mali wears a black-and-white mask on his head. Masks have always played an important part in African religious rituals, dances, and festivals.

Cape Verde Islands

Algeria	Chad	Egypt	Eritrea
Ethiopia	Libya	Mali	Morocco
Mauritania	Niger	Sudan	Tunisia

250   500   750 Kilometers

100   200   300   400   500 Miles

West Africa

The lands around the Atlantic coast and the Gulf of Guinea are hot and very humid. They are crossed by great rivers such as the Sénégal, Gambia, Volta, and Niger. Behind the sand bars and surf of the coast are forests, swamps, and fertile plantation land which produces cocoa, rubber, cotton, peanuts, and palm oil. Farther inland are plateaus and grazing lands, but in the far north the pasture is thin, and dust blows south from the Sahara. The region includes priceless mineral resources, such as oil in Nigeria, gold in Ghana, and diamonds in Sierra Leone.

Powerful empires and kingdoms grew up long ago in this part of Africa, but the arrival of Europeans in the 1500s led to a cruel trade in slaves to the Americas and a long period of rule by Great Britain and France. Independence from these colonial powers came in the 1950s, but economic and political problems followed, with periods of military rule. The largest and most powerful country in the region is Nigeria.

Cotton is an important crop in West African countries such as Guinea-Bissau, Togo, Benin, Nigeria, and Burkina Faso.

Northern West Africa is mostly Muslim, while the south is mostly Christian. This Catholic cathedral was built at Yamoussoukro, Côte d'Ivoire, in 1989. It is called Our Lady of Peace. It cost millions of dollars in a country where many people are desperately poor.

Okra stew is a popular dish in West Africa. When okra is stewed it becomes smooth and sticky. It may be served with shrimp, saltfish, hotly spiced meat, or yam chips.

The dense forests and lagoons of the Niger delta region, here at Wari, are rich in oil and are a major source of wealth for the Nigerian government. Local people have protested about the pollution of their environment by the oil companies and their lack of a share in the profits.

Togo is home to various peoples, including the Ewe, Kabre, and Mina. Many keep up their cultural traditions. These dancers from Togo wear beaded kilts, horns, necklaces, and armlets. Dance and music play an important part in life throughout Africa, and African drumming has influenced the popular music of the Americas.

Peoples and languages

West Africa is home to very many different ethnic groups, such as the Wolof, Mende, Kru, Mossi, Ewe, Hausa, Fulani, Ibo, and Yoruba. Liberia and Sierra Leone were settled in the 1800s by Africans freed from the slave trade across the Atlantic.

Many different languages are heard in West Africa, and many people can speak either English or French, the languages of the colonial period, in addition to their own tongue. Colonial languages are still used in many schools, law courts, and businesses.

Portuguese is spoken in Cape Verde and Guinea-Bissau, and Spanish in the small country of Equatorial Guinea.

This ritual dance is being performed by Cameroon's "voodoo queens". They follow African religions which believe in a world of spirits. Voodoo beliefs traveled from West Africa to the Americas in the days of the slave trade. Today about a quarter of all Cameroonians follow spirit beliefs.

A colorful textile from Benin features local animal life—a bull, a chameleon, a snake, and two fruit bats.

MAURITANIA

SENEGAL
■ Dakar

GAMBIA
Banjul ■

Bissau ■

GUINEA
BISSAU GUINEA

Conakry ■

Freetown ■

SIERRA LEONE

MALI

BURKINA
FASO

Ouagadougou ●

CÔTE
D'IVOIRE

Yamoussoukro ●

Monrovia ■

LIBERIA

Abidjan ●

GHANA

TOGO

BENIN

Lomé ●

Accra ●

Porto Novo ●

NIGER

Benue

Kano ●

Kaduna ●

Ibadan ●

NIGERIA

Niger

Abuja ■

Lagos ●

Port Harcourt ●

CHAD

CENTRAL
AFRICAN
REPUBLIC

Douala ●

BIOKO

Yaoundé ■

CAMEROON

EQUATORIAL GUINEA ■ Mbini

SÃO TOMÉ
AND PRINCIPE

■ Libreville

GABON

CONGO

ZAIRE (D.R.C.)

Brazzaville ●

ANGOLA

The president's palace in Dakar, the capital of Senegal. After the country became independent from France in 1960, it remained under the rule of President Léopold Senghor for 20 years. Today it is a democracy. The Senegalese economy depends on peanuts, fish-processing, and chemicals.

N

Crops such as corn and millet are pounded into flour with heavy pestles. Many African peoples make porridges, mashes, or drinks from these grains. West African women often lead very busy lives, cooking, working in the fields, and selling produce such as yams, peanuts, and palm oil at the market.

Benin

Cameroon

Congo

Côte d'Ivoire

Gabon

Gambia

Ghana

Guinea

Liberia

Nigeria

Senegal

Sierra Leone

Togo

Burkina Faso

Guinea-Bissau

Equatorial
Guinea

São Tomé and
Príncipe

65

Central and East Africa

The Zaire (or Congo) River drains a vast area of rain forest on its journey to the Atlantic coast. The river and the network of waterways that flow into it provide useful transport routes for riverboats and canoes. The country of Zaire lies on the Equator and has a hot and humid climate, with torrential rains and thunderstorms. It has a fertile soil and rich desposits of copper, cobalt, zinc, manganese, and diamonds. In recent years Zaire has suffered through a severe civil war. Rebel forces finally took control in 1997 and Zaire was renamed the Democratic Republic of Congo.

To the north, in the Central African Republic, the rain forest gives way to grasslands and dry plateaus. To the east are volcanic mountain ranges and the two small nations of Rwanda and Burundi, both of which have also suffered tragic civil wars.

A great crack in the Earth's crust, the Great Rift Valley, runs through East Africa. Its course is marked by mountains, gorges, and deep lakes. Uganda, Kenya, and Tanzania take in fertile highlands, savanna (grassy plains dotted with trees), and desert regions. The Indian Ocean coast is lined with white beaches, palm trees, and coral islands. East Africa produces sugarcane, mangoes, coffee, and sisal. Some people in Central and East Africa lead very traditional lives, such as the Masai who herd cattle on the grasslands of Kenya and Tanzania. Others live and work in busy, modern cities, such as Nairobi.

A garden among the rooftops on the island of Zanzibar, just north of Dar-es-Salaam. Zanzibar has been part of Tanzania since 1974, and is famous for spices, especially cloves, and for its large wooden sailing vessels called dhows.

Two women from Zaire (Dem. Rep. of Congo) exchange gossip as they braid their hair in elaborate styles. Central and East African fashions feature colorful, boldly patterned cotton wraps tied around the waist.

Kilimanjaro towers above the savanna of the Kenya-Tanzania border. At 19,340 feet above sea level, it is the highest mountain in Africa, but even in this region of burning heat, its summits are covered in snow.

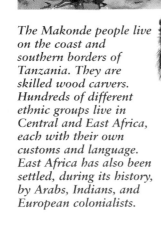

The Makonde people live on the coast and southern borders of Tanzania. They are skilled wood carvers. Hundreds of different ethnic groups live in Central and East Africa, each with their own customs and language. East Africa has also been settled, during its history, by Arabs, Indians, and European colonialists.

Lions often hunt by night, and spend the day sleeping in the shade and playing with their cubs. These big cats hunt the great herds of zebra and wildebeeste which still roam the African savanna. Many are protected within wildlife reserves.

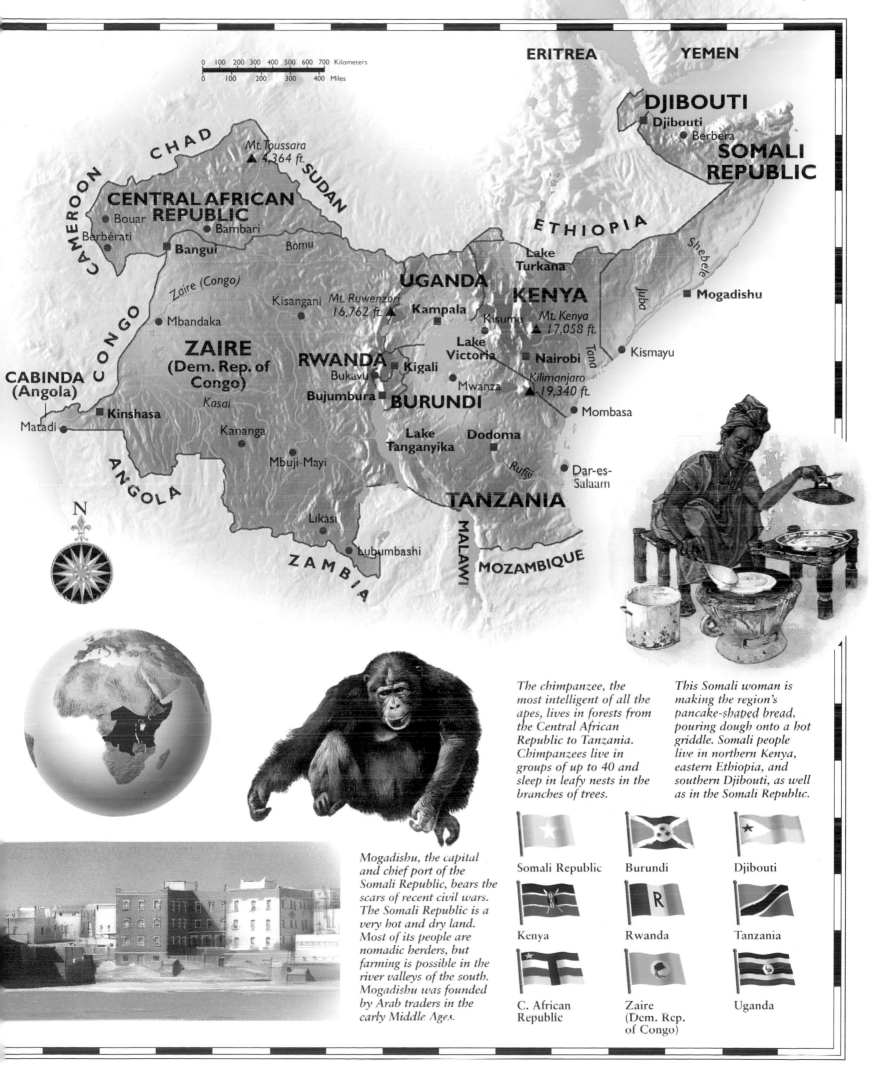

ERITREA   YEMEN

DJIBOUTI
• Djibouti
  • Berbera

SOMALI
REPUBLIC

0 100 200 300 400 500 600 700 Kilometers
0 100 200 300 400 Miles

CHAD

Mt. Toussara
▲ 4,364 ft.

CAMEROON

CENTRAL AFRICAN
REPUBLIC
• Bouar
• Berbérati   • Bambari
■ Bangui   Bomu

SUDAN

ETHIOPIA

Lake
Turkana

UGANDA   KENYA   Shebele

Zaire (Congo)   Mt. Ruwenzori
Kisangani   16,762 ft. ▲   Kampala   Mt. Kenya   ■ Mogadishu
CONGO   Kisumu   ▲ 17,058 ft.
• Mbandaka   Lake
                                        Victoria   Juba
ZAIRE   RWANDA   • Kigali Nairobi ■   • Kismayu
(Dem. Rep. of   Bukavu   Tana
Congo)   • Bujumbura   • Mwanza   Kilimanjaro
CABINDA   Kasai   ▲ 19,340 ft.
(Angola)   BURUNDI   • Mombasa
■ Kinshasa
Matadi •   • Kananga
                                   Lake   Dodoma
ANGOLA   Tanganyika   •

                    • Mbuji-Mayi   Rufiji   • Dar-es-
                                                           Salaam
N   TANZANIA
                    • Likasi

                    • Lubumbashi   MALAWI
        ZAMBIA   MOZAMBIQUE

The chimpanzee, the
most intelligent of all the
apes, lives in forests from
the Central African
Republic to Tanzania.
Chimpanzees live in
groups of up to 40 and
sleep in leafy nests in the
branches of trees.

This Somali woman is
making the region's
pancake-shaped bread,
pouring dough onto a hot
griddle. Somali people
live in northern Kenya,
eastern Ethiopia, and
southern Djibouti, as well
as in the Somali Republic.

Mogadishu, the capital
and chief port of the
Somali Republic, bears the
scars of recent civil wars.
The Somali Republic is a
very hot and dry land.
Most of its people are
nomadic herders, but
farming is possible in the
river valleys of the south.
Mogadishu was founded
by Arab traders in the
early Middle Ages.

Somali Republic   Burundi   Djibouti

Kenya   Rwanda   Tanzania

C. African
Republic

Zaire
(Dem. Rep.
of Congo)

Uganda

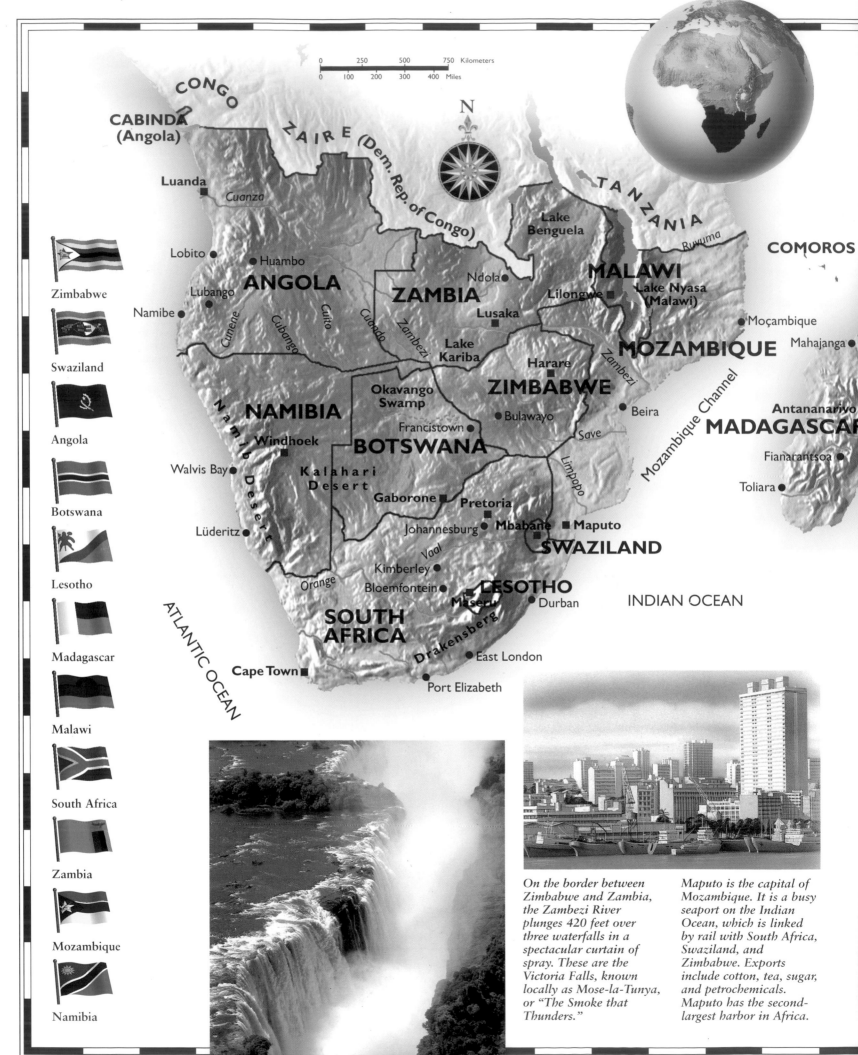

CABINDA
(Angola)

CONGO

ZAIRE (Dem. Rep. of Congo)

TANZANIA

Luanda

Cuanza

Lake
Benguela

COMOROS

Lobito

Huambo

ANGOLA

ZAMBIA

Ndola

MALAWI

Lilongwe

Lake Nyasa
(Malawi)

Moçambique

Lusaka

Mahajanga

Namibe

Lubango

Cunene

Cuito

Cubango

Cuando

Zambezi

Lake
Kariba

Harare

MOZAMBIQUE

Zambezi

NAMIBIA

Okavango
Swamp

ZIMBABWE

Bulawayo

Beira

Antananarivo

MADAGASCAR

Windhoek

BOTSWANA

Francistown

Save

Fianarantsoa

Walvis Bay

Namib Desert

Kalahari
Desert

Gaborone

Pretoria

Limpopo

Mozambique Channel

Toliara

Lüderitz

Johannesburg

Mbabane Maputo

Vaal

Kimberley

SWAZILAND

INDIAN OCEAN

Orange

Bloemfontein

LESOTHO

Maseru

Durban

ATLANTIC OCEAN

SOUTH
AFRICA

Drakensberg

East London

Cape Town

Port Elizabeth

Zimbabwe

Swaziland

Angola

Botswana

Lesotho

Madagascar

Malawi

South Africa

Zambia

Mozambique

Namibia

On the border between
Zimbabwe and Zambia,
the Zambezi River
plunges 420 feet over
three waterfalls in a
spectacular curtain of
spray. These are the
Victoria Falls, known
locally as Mose-la-Tunya,
or "The Smoke that
Thunders."

Maputo is the capital of
Mozambique. It is a busy
seaport on the Indian
Ocean, which is linked
by rail with South Africa,
Swaziland, and
Zimbabwe. Exports
include cotton, tea, sugar,
and petrochemicals.
Maputo has the second-
largest harbor in Africa.

Southern Africa

Southern Africa includes grasslands known as veld, great swamps such as the Okavango, and harsh deserts such as the Namib and Kalahari. The region has high mountains and beautiful lakes and its beaches border the southern waters of the Atlantic and Indian oceans. Africa's biggest island, Madagascar, lies across the Mozambique Channel. Southern Africa has a rich wildlife including antelope, lions, and elephants. Madagascar is famous for its lemurs.

Southern Africa produces many crops, including grapes, citrus fruits, wheat, corn, and tobacco. Cattle ranching is important for the economy of Botswana.

Peoples of the region include the Herero, Tswana, Khoi-San, Ndebele, Shona, Zulu, Xhosa, Swazi, and Sotho. Minorities are descended from Dutch, English, and Asian settlers. The most powerful and wealthy country of the region is South Africa. For many years this country was ruled by white-only governments. Black and Asian citizens were not allowed to vote. Today South Africa has become a democracy, and its first black president, Nelson Mandela, was elected in 1994.

Diamonds are mined in South Africa and Namibia. The region has very rich mineral resources, including copper in Zambia, gold in South Africa, and uranium in Namibia. The world's largest diamond was found in South Africa in 1905.

● Antseranana

● Toamasina

A Comoros woman wears white make-up made of wood ground against coral and mixed to a pulp. It protects and cleanses the skin. Comoros islanders are descended from Africans, Arabs, and Southeast Asians. The Comoros islands produce spices and exquisite oils for perfume.

This girl is carrying a load of cornhusks. Many Zambian women work long hours on small farms and garden plots where they grow corn, sorghum, millet, and a starchy root called cassava to feed their families. Other crops are grown on a larger scale for export. They include sugarcane, cotton, and tobacco.

Fruits of Zimbabwe include mangoes, passion fruit, juicy pineapples, and delicious avocados. They grow well in the country's hot, tropical climate, which is milder on the high plateaus and hills.

The forests of Madagascar were once home to a wide variety of wildlife. However, much of the island has now been stripped bare by farmers and logging companies. Without roots to hold it in place, the soil is soon washed away by tropical rains. The government has started to plant new forests to stop this from happening.

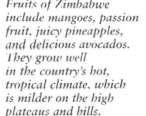

South Africa's 19th-century parliament buildings are in the southern city of Cape Town. Since 1994 they have housed a multi-racial democratic government. The largest political parties include the African National Congress, the National Party, and Inkatha Freedom Party.

There are 90 species of chameleon and most of these live in tropical Africa, including Madagascar. Chameleons are large lizards with swivelling eyes and long sticky tongues. They are able to change their color for camouflage. Their long tails and toes wrap around twigs and branches.

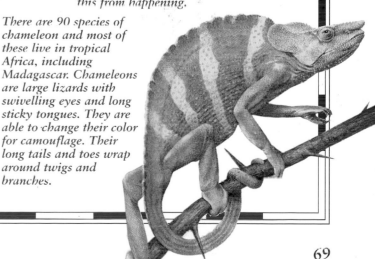

Australia

Australia

Australia is an island so huge that it is normally considered to be a continent in its own right. It stretches from the subtropical forests of the north to the cool seas of Tasmania, far to the south. Australia is bordered in the northeast by 1,259 miles of coral, the Great Barrier Reef. This is the haunt of sharks and beautiful tropical fish. While the "outback," the remote lands of the interior, is famed in Australian history, most Australians today are town-dwellers.

Eastern and southern coasts are the site of large cities such as Brisbane, Sydney, Melbourne, and Adelaide. Many rivers rise in the Great Dividing Range, which runs parallel to the coast. Inland are grasslands, largely given over to sheep stations and cattle ranches. These give way to eucalyptus forest, dry scrub, burning deserts, and rocks. Beyond the vast Nullarbor Plain is Perth, the largest city in Western Australia.

Australia became an island so long ago that many of its animals, such as kangaroos and koalas, are seen nowhere else on Earth. Aborigines, expert hunters and travelers, have lived in Australia for at least 40,000 years.

The dense rain forest of the Lamington Plateau, to the south of Brisbane, is a haven for rare animals and plants. It was made a National Park in 1915 and today is popular with bush-walkers, campers, and nature lovers.

Map

★ Darwin — Arnhem Land

Gulf of Carpentaria

Kimberley Plateau

Broome •

Fitzroy

NORTHERN TERRITORY

Barkly Tableland

Great Sandy Desert

AUSTRALIA

Ashburton

Alice Springs •

Carnarvon •

Gibson Desert

▲ Uluru (Ayers Rock) 2,844 ft.

Alberga

Simpson Desert

Lake

WESTERN AUSTRALIA

Murchison

Great Victoria Desert

SOUTHERN AUSTRALIA

Lake Eyre

Geraldton •

Nullarbor Plain

Lake Torrens

Kalgoorlie •

★ Perth
Fremantle

Great Australian Bight

N

Adelaide ★

| 0 | 100 | 200 | 300 | 400 | 500 | 600 | Kilometers |
| 0 | | 100 | | 200 | | 300 | Miles |

Surf's up! The rolling waves of the Pacific Ocean are perfect for surfing. Australia's sunny climate makes it ideal for sports and outdoor pursuits.

Boomerangs were first used for hunting by Australia's Aborigines. When thrown, the boomerang curves back toward the thrower. Aborigine crafts and bark paintings are highly valued as works of art.

A Pacific power

In 1788 the British founded a prison colony in New South Wales. Settlers then seized the land from the Aborigines, many of whom were hunted down and killed. Many more European immigrants arrived over the years. Only in recent years have Aborigines gained full rights as citizens.

Australia built its wealth on vast mineral reserves and on exports of wool and meat. Today it is one of the leading economic powers of the Pacific. Australia is still ruled by the British monarch, but there are growing calls for the country to become a republic.

Cape York Peninsula

Mitchell

Cairns

Great Barrier Reef

Norman

Townsville

Flinders

Great Dividing Range

QUEENSLAND

SOUTH PACIFIC OCEAN

amarrinda

Rockhampton

Narrego

Brisbane

Sydney Harbor is known for two famous landmarks—its opera house and its bridge. The skyscrapers belong to the city's business district, which borders the green spaces of the Royal Botanic Garden.

Darling

NEW SOUTH WALES

Great Dividing Range

Lachlan

Newcastle

★Sydney

Murray

■CANBERRA (A.C.T.)

VICTORIA ▲ *Mt. Kosciusko 7,310 ft.*

★Melbourne

Canberra is Australia's purpose-built capital. Its new parliament buildings, on Capital Hill, were opened in 1988. Australia is governed on a federal basis, with some of its laws being passed nationally and others regionally by its eight states and territories.

Australian Aborigines play the didgeridoo, a long, hollow wooden instrument which makes a deep, droning, whirring sound.

Lamingtons are cake squares coated in chocolate and coconut— a tasty snack. Australia's many different immigrants have brought their own styles of cooking with them, whether Greek, Italian, or Thai.

Bass Strait

TASMANIA

★Hobart

New Zealand

The beautiful islands of New Zealand lie in the southwest Pacific Ocean, about 1,000 miles from Australia. They have a mild, often cool, climate.

North Island is the most populated part of the country. Here are the two large cities of Auckland and Wellington. This is a land of fertile plains, rising to a central plateau and eastern mountains. The island has three active volcanoes in addition to bubbling hot springs and spectacular geysers (gushers of water heated by volcanic rocks, deep under the ground).

Across Cook Strait is South Island, with its high ridge of mountains, the Southern Alps. Mount Cook is 12,349 miles above sea level. Over the ages glaciers have scraped out deep sea inlets in the southwest. To the east are the fertile Canterbury Plains and the hills of Otago. The chief southern cities are Christchurch and Dunedin. To the south again lies mountainous Stewart Island, across the Foveaux Strait, and to the east are the Chatham Islands.

New Zealand's unspoiled coasts and mountains are ideal for outdoor pursuits such as sailing and climbing. New Zealanders are keen sports enthusiasts and are world leaders at rugby football.

Tuataras are large, lizard-like creatures, the only surviving members of their reptile family. They were once common in New Zealand but now are found only on a few islands off the coast. They live in burrows and hunt insects by night. Unlike most reptiles, tuataras can remain active in temperatures as low as 45°F.

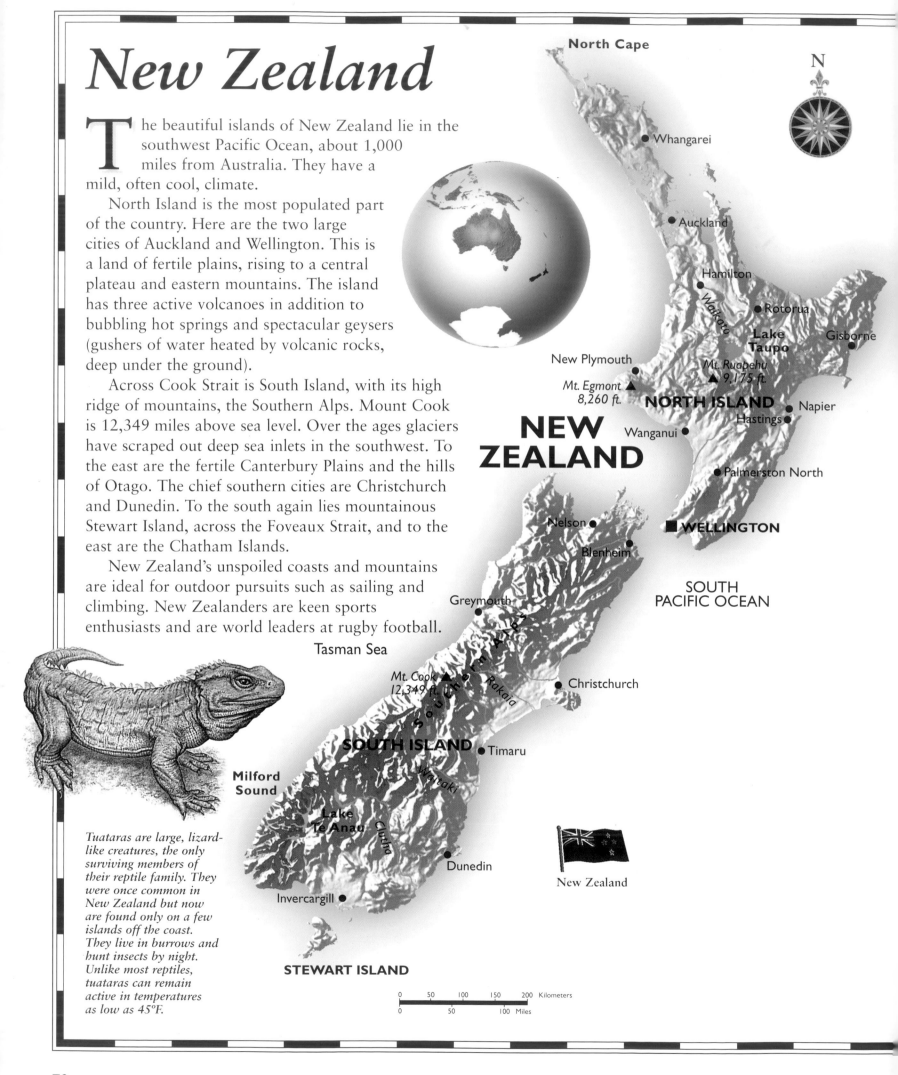

North Cape

N

Whangarei

Auckland

Hamilton

Waikato

Rotorua

Lake Taupo

Gisborne

New Plymouth

Mt. Ruapehu
▲ 9,175 ft.

Mt. Egmont ▲
8,260 ft.

NORTH ISLAND

Napier

Hastings

NEW ZEALAND

Wanganui

Palmerston North

Nelson

Blenheim

■ WELLINGTON

SOUTH PACIFIC OCEAN

Greymouth

SOUTHERN ALPS

Tasman Sea

Mt. Cook ▲
12,349 ft.

Rakaia

Christchurch

SOUTH ISLAND

Timaru

Milford Sound

Waitaki

Lake Te Anau

Clutha

Dunedin

New Zealand

Invercargill

STEWART ISLAND

0   50   100   150   200   Kilometers
0   50   100 Miles

A geyser bursts into the air at Whaka-rewarewa, near Rotorua on North Island. The energy from New Zealand's hot rocks is harnessed to generate electric power. Geysers and hot springs also attract tourists who are fascinated by the forces of nature.

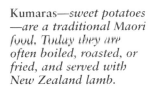

Kumaras—sweet potatoes—are a traditional Maori food. Today they are often boiled, roasted, or fried, and served with New Zealand lamb.

The flightless kiwi is an emblem of New Zealand. With its long bill it hunts for insects among fallen leaves in the forest. New Zealand has no native mammals, and so its birds never needed to fly away from attack.

Peoples of the islands

The first New Zealanders were the Maoris, a Polynesian people who settled the islands from about A.D. 800 onward. They hunted moas, the large flightless birds which then lived there, collected shellfish, grew sweet potatoes, and built forts called *pa*. New Zealand became a British colony in 1840.

The Maoris were soon cheated of their lands by the European settlers who rushed to New Zealand when gold was discovered in 1861. New Zealand became independent in 1907, but retained strong links with Britain. In the past 20 years it has seen itself more as one of the Pacific trading nations.

Most New Zealanders are English-speakers of European descent. Maoris make up about 10 percent of the population, and there are other Polynesian settlers such as Cook Islanders. Farming is the mainstay of the economy. Major exports include wool and lamb, butter and cheese, and apples and pears.

Wellington is the New Zealand capital. It is a seaport, built on the southwestern tip of North Island. It is also a center for business and communications, and manufactures machinery, chemicals, soap, and vehicles.

New Zealand has many fast-flowing rivers and large lakes, filled by melting snows. They are used to generate electricity. Three-quarters of all power comes from the country's 30 hydroelectric schemes. Lake Roxburgh in the Otago region of South Island has been dammed so that its waters can drive powerful turbines. New Zealand also uses coal, oil, natural gas, geothermal energy, and natural steam in its power stations.

Farming is an essential part of the New Zealand economy. For every person who lives there, there are thought to be 20 animals. Sheep like those shown here on a farm in Cambridge, North Island, are the most important livestock. New Zealand lamb and wool are famous throughout the world.

Giant wetas are huge, flightless crickets. There are various species. They have been hunted by rats and other rodents brought to New Zealand by human beings, and are now only found on some offshore islands.

Pacific Islands

The Pacific Ocean is the largest expanse of water in the world, covering an area of about 63,838,000 square miles. It has deep sea trenches, volcanic islands, and coral reefs.

The settlement of the scattered island chains of the Pacific was an amazing feat of sailing and exploration, which took place between 4,000 and 1,000 years ago. Inhabitants of the region today include Melanesians, Micronesians, Polynesians and groups of European or Asian descent. Many islanders have kept up ancient customs and traditions, such as dancing, singing, the weaving of garlands, and public feasting.

Many of the Pacific islands came under foreign rule in the 1700s and 1800s. Since the 1960s some of these have formed new, independent nations such as Kiribati, Tuvalu, and Vanuatu. Many Pacific islanders live by fishing and growing tropical fruits, coconuts, and root crops such as taro. Most of the islands are very beautiful and some attract tourists. Others, however, have been stripped by phosphate mining or blasted by the testing of nuclear weapons.

Papua New Guinea, which shares its island home with Irian Jaya, the easternmost province of Indonesia, has valuable copper reserves on Bougainville, and its warm, humid climate is ideal for growing timber, cocoa, and coffee. The French territory of New Caledonia also has rich mineral reserves, but most Pacific islands have little land or resources.

Pago Pago is a port of call for Pacific shipping and the heart of the fishing industry. Sited on Tutuila island, it is the capital of American Samoa. Here, fishing crews are unloading a catch of tuna, bound for the island's seafood canneries.

This dish, known as unu bona boroma, is eaten in Papua New Guinea. It is made from boiled slices of breadfruit served with bacon, onions, and chicken stock.

The world's largest butterfly is the rare Queen Alexandra's birdwing of Papua New Guinea. It lives in rain forests in the north. The wingspan of females may be a staggering 11 inches or more.

East China Sea

WAKE ISLAND (U.S.A.)

NORTHERN MARIANA ISLANDS (U.S.A.)

Philippine Sea

GUAM (U.S.A.)

PALAU

FEDERATED STATES OF MICRONESIA

NAURU

IRIAN JAYA (INDONESIA)

PAPUA NEW GUINEA

SOLOMON ISLANDS

Arafura Sea

Port Moresby

VANUATU

Coral Sea

NEW CALEDONIA (Fr.)

AUSTRALIA

Tasman Sea

N

NEW ZEALAND

Micronesia

Marshall Islands

Fiji

Kiribati

Tuvalu

Nauru

Vanuatu

Papua New Guinea

Western Samoa

Palau

Solomon Islands

Tonga

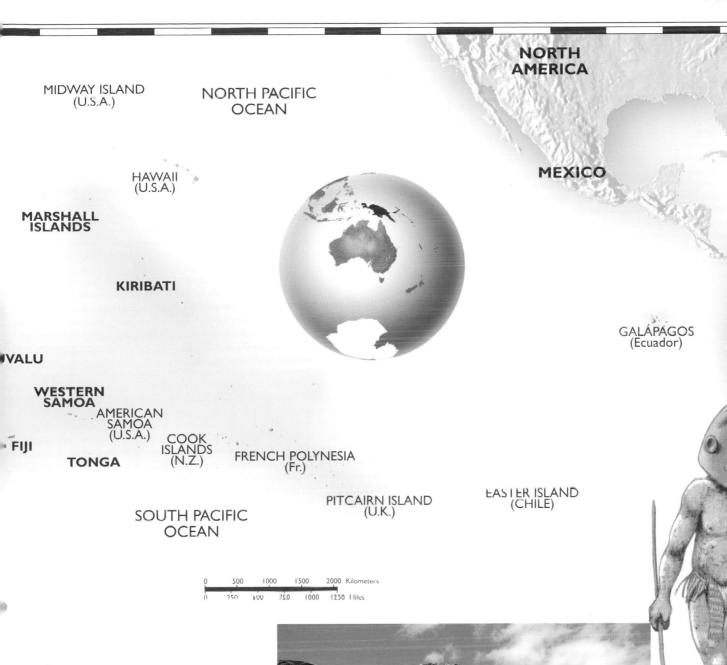

NORTH
AMERICA

MIDWAY ISLAND
(U.S.A.)

NORTH PACIFIC
OCEAN

MEXICO

HAWAII
(U.S.A.)

**MARSHALL
ISLANDS**

KIRIBATI

GALÁPAGOS
(Ecuador)

SOUTH
AMERICA

VALU

**WESTERN
SAMOA**

AMERICAN
SAMOA
(U.S.A.)

FIJI

COOK
ISLANDS
(N.Z.)

FRENCH POLYNESIA
(Fr.)

TONGA

PITCAIRN ISLAND
(U.K.)

EASTER ISLAND
(CHILE)

SOUTH PACIFIC
OCEAN

0   500   1000   1500   2000 Kilometers
0   250   500   750   1000   1250 Miles

Huge statues (right) called moai *were raised on Easter Island about 1,000 years ago. The island was the home of Polynesian people, who believed that the statues had mysterious powers. Today, Easter Island is governed by Chile, 2,484 miles to the east.*

A craftsman (left) carves a tiki, *a stone figure from one of the myths of the ancient Polynesians. He comes from the island of Nuku Hiva, one of the Marquesas chain in French Polynesia. Traditional crafts include carving in stone, wood, and whalebone.*

A villager from the Goroka region of Papua New Guinea wears a mud mask in the image of an evil spirit. The masks were once worn to scare enemies, but today are worn only at feasts.

A woman from Kiribati, in the central Pacific, puts together strips of matting made from fronds of the coconut palm. Coconuts provide food, fiber, and roofing materials. They are dried to make copra, one of the Pacific region's most important exports.

The Polar Lands

The northernmost and southernmost points on Earth are called the Poles. Around them are bitterly cold, permanently frozen lands, swept by icy winds. While it is winter at the North Pole, it is summer at the South Pole. Polar summers are short, with no actual darkness, while the winters are long, with little daylight. The skies sometimes flicker with glowing lights called "aurorae."

Antarctica is the fifth largest continent. It is a land of mountains and glaciers, white with dazzling snow and ice. Even the sea is frozen solid. In places the Antarctic ice sheet is nearly 3 miles thick. Great flat-topped icebergs break off from the ice shelf and drift through the Southern Ocean. Antarctica is the windiest place on Earth and has some of the lowest temperatures on record. Birds nest on the icy coasts and fish and whales swim offshore, but no mammals live on the frozen lands around the South Pole.

No people live here permanently. There are bases visited by teams of scientists. Several countries claim territories in Antarctica, and the land is rich in minerals. However, more and more people are calling for Antarctica to be left unspoiled, the last true wilderness on Earth.

Melting ice floats off the shores of Antarctica. Some scientists believe that the Earth's climate is becoming warmer. If the polar ice sheets melted, sea levels would rise around the world and cause flooding.

The Emperor penguin is one of six penguin species that breed in Antarctica. Its sleek coat protects it against the bitterly cold waters where it catches fish.

The first person to reach the South Pole was the Norwegian explorer Roald Amundsen, on December 14, 1911. He used dogs to pull sleds of supplies across the ice.

SOUTH ATLANTIC OCEAN

INDIAN OCEAN

SOUTH PACIFIC OCEAN

Antarctic Peninsula

Queen Maud Land

Enderby Land

Weddell Sea

Ronne Ice Shelf

Trans-Antarctic Mountains

▲ Vinson Massif 16,864 ft.

● South Pole

Ellsworth Land

Ross Ice Shelf

Wilkes Land

▲ Mt. Erebus 12,448 ft.

Victoria Land

Ross Sea

Antarctic Circle

0 200 400 600 800 1000 1200 1400 Kilometers
0   200   400   600   800 Miles

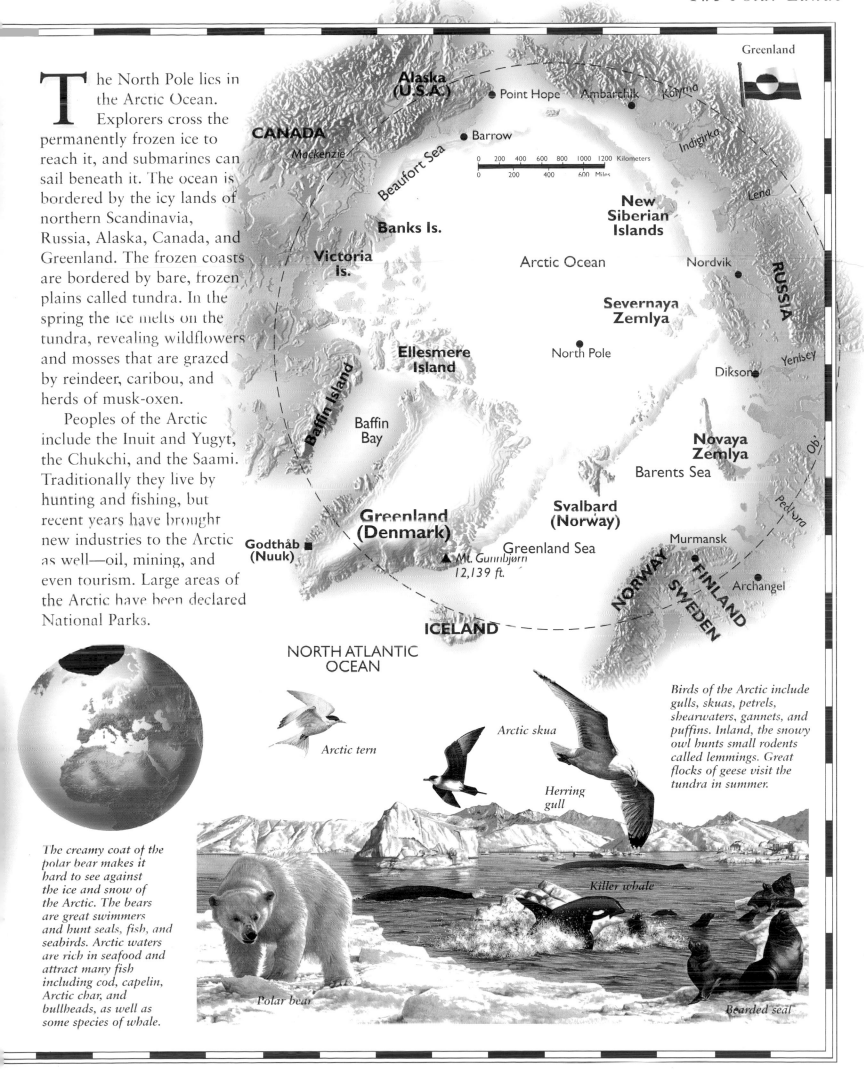

The North Pole lies in the Arctic Ocean. Explorers cross the permanently frozen ice to reach it, and submarines can sail beneath it. The ocean is bordered by the icy lands of northern Scandinavia, Russia, Alaska, Canada, and Greenland. The frozen coasts are bordered by bare, frozen plains called tundra. In the spring the ice melts on the tundra, revealing wildflowers and mosses that are grazed by reindeer, caribou, and herds of musk-oxen.

Peoples of the Arctic include the Inuit and Yugyt, the Chukchi, and the Saami. Traditionally they live by hunting and fishing, but recent years have brought new industries to the Arctic as well—oil, mining, and even tourism. Large areas of the Arctic have been declared National Parks.

Greenland

Alaska (U.S.A.) • Point Hope   Ambarchik   Kolyma

CANADA   • Barrow   Indigirka

Mackenzie   Beaufort Sea   Lena

Banks Is.   New Siberian Islands

Arctic Ocean   Nordvik   RUSSIA

Victoria Is.   Severnaya Zemlya   Yenisey

North Pole   Dikson

Ellesmere Island

Baffin Island   Novaya Zemlya

Baffin Bay   Barents Sea   Ob

Greenland (Denmark)   Svalbard (Norway)   Murmansk

Godthåb (Nuuk)   Greenland Sea   Pechora

▲ Mt. Gunnbjørn 12,139 ft.   NORWAY   FINLAND   SWEDEN   Archangel

ICELAND

NORTH ATLANTIC OCEAN

Birds of the Arctic include gulls, skuas, petrels, shearwaters, gannets, and puffins. Inland, the snowy owl hunts small rodents called lemmings. Great flocks of geese visit the tundra in summer.

Arctic tern

Arctic skua

Herring gull

Killer whale

The creamy coat of the polar bear makes it hard to see against the ice and snow of the Arctic. The bears are great swimmers and hunt seals, fish, and seabirds. Arctic waters are rich in seafood and attract many fish including cod, capelin, Arctic char, and bullheads, as well as some species of whale.

Polar bear

Bearded seal

North America

Facts and Figures

Country	Area (sq. miles)	Population	Capital	Official language	Currency	Major products
Antigua and Barbuda	170	62,000	St. John's	English	East Caribbean dollar	Oil products
Bahamas	5,353	262,000	Nassau	English	Bahamian dollar	Oil products
Barbados	166	259,000	Bridgetown	English	East Caribbean dollar	Sugar, oil products, electrical goods, clothing
Belize	8,867	198,000	Belmopan	English, Spanish	Belize dollar	Sugar, bananas, citrus products, fish, clothing
Canada	3,850,789	27,445,000	Ottawa	English, French	Canadian dollar	Wheat, natural gas, oil, wood pulp, newsprint, iron ore, cars and parts, fish
Costa Rica	19,730	3,099,000	San José	Spanish	Colon	Coffee, bananas, manufactured goods
Cuba	42,806	10,822,000	Havana	Spanish	Peso	Sugar, tobacco
Dominica	290	72,000	Roseau	English	East Caribbean dollar	Citrus fruits, bananas
Dominican Republic	18,704	7,471,000	Santo Domingo	Spanish	Peso	Sugar, coffee
El Salvador	8,125	5,396,000	San Salvador	Spanish	Colon	Coffee, cotton
Grenada	131	91,000	St. George's	English	East Caribbean dollar	Cocoa, nutmeg, mace, bananas
Guatemala	42,045	9,745,000	Guatemala City	Spanish	Quetzal	Coffee, bananas, cotton, beef
Haiti	10,715	6,764,000	Port-au-Prince	French	Gourde	Coffee, bauxite, sugar
Honduras	43,277	5,462,000	Tegucigalpa	Spanish	Lempira	Coffee, bananas, timber, meat
Jamaica	4,412	2,469,000	Kingston	English	Jamaican dollar	Bauxite, alumina
Mexico	759,530	89,538,000	Mexico City	Spanish	Peso	Oil, coffee, cotton, sugar, manufactured goods
Nicaragua	50,456	4,130,000	Managua	Spanish	Cordoba	Cotton, coffee, meat, chemicals
Panama	29,764	2,515,000	Panama	Spanish	Balboa	Bananas, shrimps, sugar, oil products
St. Kitts (St. Christopher) and Nevis	101	42,000	Basseterre	English	East Caribbean dollar	Sugar
St. Lucia	238	137,000	Castries	English	East Caribbean dollar	Bananas, cocoa, citrus fruits, coconuts, tourism

Country	Area (sq. miles)	Population	Capital	Official language	Currency	Major products
St. Vincent and the Grenadines	150	109,000	Kingstown	English	East Caribbean dollar	Bananas, arrowroot, coconuts
Trinidad and Tobago	1,981	1,265,000	Port-of-Spain	English	Trinidad dollar	Oil, asphalt, chemicals, sugar, fruit, cocoa, coffee
United States of America	3,536,278	255,020,000	Washington D.C.	English	U.S. dollar	Machinery, vehicles, aircraft and parts, iron and steel goods, coal, chemicals, cereals, soybeans, textiles, cotton

South America

Facts and Figures

Country	Area (sq. miles)	Population	Capital	Official language	Currency	Major products
Argentina	1,073,394	33,101,000	Buenos Aires	Spanish	Peso	Meat and meat products, tobacco, textiles, leather, machinery
Bolivia	424,162	7,832,000	La Paz (Seat of government); Sucre (Legal capital)	Spanish	Boliviano	Tin, oil, natural gas, cotton
Brazil	3,285,620	156,275,000	Brasilia	Portuguese	Real	Machinery, vehicles, soybeans, coffee, cocoa
Chile	284,520	13,599,000	Santiago	Spanish	Peso	Wood pulp, paper, copper, timber, iron ore, nitrates
Colombia	440,830	33,424,000	Bogota	Spanish	Peso	Coffee, emeralds, sugar, oil, meat, skins and hides
Ecuador	109,483	10,741,000	Quito	Spanish	Sucre	Oil, bananas, cocoa, coffee
French Guiana	32,255	104,000	Cayenne	French	French franc	Bauxite, shrimp, bananas
Guyana	83,000	808,000	Georgetown	English	Guyanese dollar	Sugar, rice, bauxite, alumina, timber
Paraguay	157,047	4,519,000	Asuncion	Spanish	Guarani	Cotton, soybeans, tobacco, timber
Peru	480,418	22,454,000	Lima	Spanish	Sol	Metals, minerals (silver, lead, zinc, copper), fish
Suriname	63,022	438,000	Paramaribo	Dutch, English	Guilder	Bauxite, alumina, rice, citrus fruit
Uruguay	68,041	3,131,000	Montevideo	Spanish	Peso	Meat, wool, hides and skins
Venezuela	352,143	20,249,000	Caracas	Spanish	Bolívar	Oil, iron, cocoa, coffee

Europe

Facts and Figures

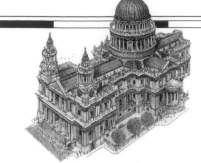

Country	Area (sq. miles)	Population	Capital	Official language	Currency	Major products
Albania	11,100	3,363,000	Tirana	Albanian	Lek	Oil, bitumen, metals, tobacco, fruit and vegetables
Andorra	175	47,000	Andorra la Vella	Catalan	French franc	Tourism, postage stamps
Austria	32,380	7,884,000	Vienna	German	Schilling	Food, iron and steel, textiles, paper products, machinery
Belarus	80,160	10,321,000	Minsk	Belorussian, Russian	Ruble	Trucks and tractors, fertilizers, flax, computers
Belgium	11,788	9,998,000	Brussels	Flemish, French	Belgian franc	Chemicals, vehicles, machinery, iron, steel
Bosnia-Herzegovina	19,742	4,397,000	Sarajevo	Serbo-Croat	Dinar	Timber, textiles, corn, wheat, barley, bauxite, iron ore, coal
Bulgaria	42,858	8,963,000	Sofia	Bulgarian	Lev	Metals, machinery, textiles, tobacco, food
Croatia	21,831	4,808,000	Zagreb	Serbo-Croat	Kuna	Chemicals, textiles, aluminum products, paper, wine, bauxite
Czech Republic	30,452	10,404,000	Prague	Czech	Koruna	Machinery, timber, wheat, beer, animals, coal, uranium
Denmark	16,633	5,170,000	Copenhagen	Danish	Krone	Food, machinery, metals and metal goods
Estonia	17,376	1,542,000	Tallinn	Estonian	Kroon	Textiles, shipbuilding, mining equipment, dairy products
Finland	130,128	5,042,000	Helsinki	Finnish, Swedish	Markka	Wood and wood pulp, paper, paperboard, machinery
France	210,025	57,372,000	Paris	French	French franc	Cars, electrical equipment, wine, cereals, textiles, leather goods, chemicals, iron, steel
Germany	137,735	80,569,000	Berlin	German	Deutsch-mark	Manufactured goods, chemicals, consumer goods, engineering goods
Greece	50,953	10,300,000	Athens	Greek	Drachma	Manufactured goods, food, wine, tobacco, chemicals
Hungary	35,922	10,313,000	Budapest	Hungarian	Forint	Transport equipment, electrical goods, bauxite
Iceland	39,771	260,000	Reykjavik	Icelandic	Krona	Fish products
Ireland, Republic of	27,119	3,547,000	Dublin	English, Irish	Irish pound (punt)	Meat and meat products, dairy products, beer, whisky
Italy	116,332	57,782,000	Rome	Italian	Lira	Machinery, motor vehicles, iron and steel, textiles, shoes
Latvia	24,712	2,632,000	Riga	Latvian	Lats	Electric railway cars, telephone exchanges, dairy produce

Country	Area (sq. miles)	Population	Capital	Official language	Currency	Major products
Liechtenstein	62	28,000	Vaduz	German	Swiss franc	Cotton yarn and material, screws, bolts, needles
Lithuania	25,098	3,759,000	Vilnius	Lithuanian	Litas	Cattle, electric motors and appliances, cereals
Luxembourg	999	390,000	Luxembourg City	French, Letze-buergesch	Luxembourg franc	Iron and steel, chemicals, vehicles, machinery
Macedonia	9,919	2,050,000	Skopie	Macedonian	Denar	Chemicals, machinery, food
Malta	122	359,000	Valletta	Maltese, English	Maltese pound	Food, manufactured goods, ship repairing, tourism
Moldova	13,013	4,394,000	Chişinău	Romanian	Leu	Machinery, food processing, vines, fruit and vegetables
Monaco	0.7	28,000	Monte Carlo	French	French franc	Tourism
Netherlands	16,034	15,178,000	Amsterdam	Dutch	Guilder	Oil, chemicals, food and animals, machinery
Norway	125,181	4,286,000	Oslo	Norwegian	Krone	Animal products, paper, fish, metals, metal products, oil
Poland	120,727	38,365,000	Warsaw	Polish	Zloty	Lignite, coal, coke, iron and steel, ships, textiles, food
Portugal (inc. Azores and Madeira)	35,828	9,846,000	Lisbon	Portuguese	Escudo	Textiles, timber, cork, wine, machinery, chemicals, sardines
Romania	91,699	23,185,000	Bucharest	Romanian	Leu	Food, machinery, minerals, metals, oil, gas, chemicals
Russia	6,592,857	149,469,000	Moscow	Russian	Ruble	Wheat, timber, oil, textiles, minerals, metals, coal, gas
San Marino	24	23,000	San Marino	Italian	Italian lira	Wine, cereals, cattle, tourism, postage stamps
Slovakia	18,934	5,287,000	Bratislava	Slovak	Koruna	Manufactured goods, corn, wheat, timber, iron ore
Slovenia	7,820	1,985,000	Ljubljana	Slovenian	Tolar	Textiles, steel, wheat, potatoes, mercury, coal
Spain	208,800	38,085,000	Madrid	Spanish	Peseta	Manufactured goods, chemicals, textiles, leather, fish, wine, fruit
Sweden	173,731	8,678,000	Stockholm	Swedish	Swedish krona	Timber, machinery, metals, metal products, cars
Switzerland	15,881	6,905,000	Bern	French, German, Italian, Romansh	Swiss franc	Tourism, machinery, chemicals and pharmaceuticals, watches, food, textiles
Ukraine	233,107	52,200,000	Kiev	Ukrainian	Hryvna	Iron and steel, machinery, vehicles, sugar, coal, iron ore
United Kingdom	93,620	57,848,000	London	English	Pound sterling	Manufactured goods, electrical engineering, textiles, chemicals
Vatican City State	0.15	1000	Vatican City	Italian, Latin	Italian lira	
Yugoslavia (Serbia & Montenegro)	39,452	19,394,000	Belgrade	Serbo-Croat	Dinar	Chemicals, clothing, food, iron and steel, machinery

Asia

Facts and Figures

Country	Area (sq. miles)	Population	Capital	Official language	Currency	Major products
Afghanistan	251,772	19,062,000	Kabul	Pashtu, Dari (Persian)	Afghani	Skins, cotton, natural gas, fruit
Armenia	11,506	3,677,000	Yerevan	Armenian	Dram	Fruit and vegetables, tobacco, electrical engineering, tools
Azerbaijan	33,439	7,237,000	Baku	Azerbaijani	Manat	Cotton, grain, oil, chemicals, oil machinery
Bahrain	266	533,000	Manama	Arabic	Dinar	Oil
Bangladesh	57,299	119,288,000	Dhaka	Bengali	Taka	Jute, leather, hide and skins, tea
Bhutan	17,955	1,612,000	Thimphu	Dzongkha, Nepali, English	Ngultrum	Rice, fruit, timber
Brunei	2,226	270,000	Bandar Seri Begawan	Malay	Brunei dollar	Oil
Cambodia	69,898	9,054,000	Phnom Penh	Khmer	Riel	Rice, rubber
China	3,696,100	1,187,997,000	Beijing (Peking)	Chinese (Mandarin)	Yuan	Industrial and agricultural products
Cyprus	3,572	716,000	Nicosia	Greek, Turkish	Pound	Fruit, vegetables, wine, manufactured goods, minerals
Georgia	26,913	5,482,000	Tbilisi	Georgian	Lary	Metallurgy, machinery, citrus fruit, electrical engineering, tea
Hong Kong	403	5,800,000	Victoria	Chinese (Cantonese), English	Hong Kong dollar	Light manufactured goods, textiles, electronics
India	1,222,332	879,000,000	New Delhi	Hindi, English	Rupee	Tea, industrial goods, jute, textiles
Indonesia	741,097	191,170,000	Jakarta	Bahasa (Indonesian)	Rupiah	Oil, palm products, rubber, coffee
Iran	636,293	56,964,000	Tehran	Persian (Farsi)	Rial	Oil, natural gas, cotton
Iraq	169,234	19,290,000	Baghdad	Arabic	Iraqi dinar	Oil, dates, wool, cotton
Israel	8,473	4,946,000	Jerusalem	Hebrew, Arabic	Shekel	Cut diamonds, chemicals, fruit, tobacco
Japan	145,840	124,336,000	Tokyo	Japanese	Yen	Optical equipment, ships, vehicles, machinery, electronic goods, chemicals, textiles
Jordan	35,478	4,291,000	Amman	Arabic	Jordanian dinar	Phosphates, fruit, vegetables
Kazakhstan	1,049,154	17,038,000	Almaty	Kazakh	Tenge	Wheat, cotton, oil, gas, coal
Korea, North	47,402	22,618,000	Pyongyang	Korean	Won	Iron and other metal ores

Country	Area (sq. miles)	Population	Capital	Official language	Currency	Major products
Korea, South	38,333	43,663,000	Seoul	Korean	Won	Textiles, manufactured goods, chemicals
Kuwait	6,880	1,970,000	Kuwait City	Arabid	Kuwait dinar	Oil, chemicals
Kyrgyzstan	76,647	4,533,000	Bishkek	Kyrgyz	Som	Sheep, wool, horses, yaks, silk, electrical engineering, carpet
Laos	91,428	4,469,000	Vientiane	Lao	Kip	Timber, coffee
Lebanon	4,016	2,838,000	Beirut	Arabic	Lebanese pound	Precious metals, gemstones
Macao	6	374,000	Macao	Portuguese, Chinese	Pataca	Light manufactured goods
Malaysia	127,250	18,181,000	Kuala Lumpur	Malay	Malaysian dollar	Rubber, tin, palm oil, timber
Maldive Islands	116	231,000	Male	Divehi	Rupee	Fish, copra
Mongolia	604,826	2,310,000	Ulan Bator	Mongolian	Tugrik	Cattle, horses, wool, hair
Myanmar (Burma)	261,226	43,668,000	Yangon (Rangoon)	Burmese	Burmese kyat	Teak, oil cake, rubber, jute
Nepal	54,366	20,577,000	Katmandu	Nepali	Rupee	Grains, hides, cattle, timber
Oman	119,500	1,637,000	Muscat	Arabic	Omani riyal	Oil, dates, limes, tobacco, frankincense
Pakistan	307,373	115,520,000	Islamabad	Urdu, English	Rupee	Cotton, carpets, leather, rice
Philippines	115,830	64,259,000	Manila	Filipino	Peso	Sugar, timber, coconut products
Qatar	4,416	453,000	Doha	Arabic	Qatar riyal	Oil
Saudi Arabia	849,400	15,922,000	Riyadh	Arabic	Riyal	Oil
Singapore	248	2,812,000	Singapore	Malay, Chinese, Tamil, English	Singapore dollar	Refined oil products, electronic goods, rubber
Sri Lanka	25,334	17,405,000	Colombo	Sinhala	Rupee	Tea, rubber, coconut products, industrial goods
Syria	71,504	12,958,000	Damascus	Arabic	Syrian pound	Cotton, oil, cereals, animals
Taiwan	13,970	20,300,000	Taipei	Chinese (Mandarin)	Taiwan dollar	Textiles, electrical goods, plastics, machinery, food
Tajikistan	52,255	5,568,000	Dushanbe	Tajik	Rouble	cotton, vines, silk, carpets, aluminum
Thailand	198,113	57,760,000	Bangkok	Thai	Baht	Rice, tapioca, rubber, tin
Turkey	301,380	58,775,000	Ankara	Turkish	Turkish lira	Cotton, tobacco, nuts, fruit
Turkmenistan	188,456	3,859,000	Ashgabat	Turkmen	Manat	Cattle, sheep, lambskins, carpets, oil refining, gas
United Arab Emirates	32,302	1,629,000	Abu Dhabi	Arabic	Dirham	Oil, natural gas

Country	Area (sq. miles)	Population	Capital	Official language	Currency	Major products
Uzbekistan	172,741	21,363,000	Tashkent	Uzbek	Som	Chemicals, gas, cotton
Vietnam	127,242	69,306,000	Hanoi	Vietnamese	Dong	Fish, coal, agricultural goods
Yemen	205,000	9,400,000	San'a	Arabic	Dinar	Cotton, coffee, hides and skins, fish, refined oil

Africa

Facts and Figures

Country	Area (sq. miles)	Population	Capital	Official language	Currency	Major products
Algeria	919,591	26,346,000	Algiers	Arabic	Algerian dinar	Natural gas, oil
Angola	481,351	10,609,000	Luanda	Portuguese	Kwanza	Coffee, diamonds, oil
Benin	43,486	4,918,000	Porto Novo	French	Franc CFA	Cocoa, cotton
Botswana	224,606	1,373,000	Gaborone	English, Setswana	Pula	Copper, diamonds, meat
Burkina Faso	105,946	9,490,000	Ouagadougou	French	Franc CFA	Livestock, peanuts, cotton
Burundi	10,748	5,786,000	Bujumbura	French, Kirundi	Burundi franc	Coffee
Cameroon	183,568	12,198,000	Yaounde	English, French	Franc CFA	Cocoa, coffee, oil
Cape Verde Islands	1,557	384,000	Praia	Portuguese	Escudo	Bananas, fish
Central African Republic	240,323	3,173,000	Bangui	French	Franc CFA	Coffee, diamonds, timber
Chad	495,753	5,961,000	N'Djamena	French	Franc CFA	Cotton, cattle, meat
Comoros	719	585,000	Moroni	French	Franc CFA	Spices
Congo	132,046	2,368,000	Brazzaville	French	Franc CFA	Oil, timber
Côte d'Ivoire	124,503	12,910,000	Yamoussoukro	French	Franc CFA	Cocoa, coffee, timber
Djibouti	8,958	467,000	Djibouti	French	Djibouti franc	Cattle, hides and skins
Egypt	386,690	55,163,000	Cairo	Arabic	Egyptian pound	Cotton, oil, textiles
Equatorial Guinea	10,831	369,000	Malabo	Spanish	Franc CFA	Cocoa, coffee, timber
Eritrea	36,172	3,318,000	Asmera	No official language	Ethiopian birr in use	Hides, salt, cement
Ethiopia	446,951	50,527,000	Addis Ababa	Amharic	Birr	Coffee, hides and skins
Gabon	103,346	1,237,000	Libreville	French	Franc CFA	Manganese, oil
Gambia	4,361	878,000	Banjul	English	Dalasi	Peanuts
Ghana	92,100	15,959,000	Accra	English	Cedi	Cocoa, gold, timber

Country	Area (sq. miles)	Population	Capital	Official language	Currency	Major products
Guinea	94,925	6,116,000	Conakry	French	Guinean franc	Alumina, bauxite
Guinea-Bissau	13,949	1,006,000	Bissau	Portuguese	Guinea-Bissau-peso	Fish, peanuts
Kenya	224,960	26,985,000	Nairobi	English, Swahili	Kenya shilling	Coffee, tea, hides
Lesotho	11,721	1,836,000	Maseru	English, Sesotho	Loti	Wool, mohair
Liberia	38,253	2,580,000	Monrovia	English	Liberian dollar	Iron ore, rubber
Libya	679,359	4,875,000	Tripoli	Arabic	Libyan dinar	Oil
Madagascar	229,355	12,827,000	Antananarive	French, Malagasy	Malgache franc	Coffee, spices, vanilla
Malawi	45,750	8,823,000	Lilongwe	English, Chichewa	Kwacha	Tobacco, tea
Mali	478,839	9,818,000	Bamako	French	Mali franc	Peanuts, cotton
Mauritania	397,954	2,143,000	Nouakchott	Arabic, French	Ouguiya	Iron ore, copper
Mauritius	788	1,084,000	Port Louis	English	Rupee	Sugar, tea, tobacco
Morocco	177,116	26,318,000	Rabat	Arabic	Dirham	Phosphates, fruit
Mozambique	308,640	14,872,000	Maputo	Portuguese	Metical	Sugar, fruit, vegetables
Namibia	318,250	1,534,000	Windhoek	English	Rand	Minerals, diamonds, fish
Niger	489,190	8,252,000	Niamey	French	Franc CFA	Peanuts, livestock, uranium
Nigeria	356,670	115,664,000	Abuja	English	Naira	Oil, palm kernels, cocoa
Rwanda	10,170	7,526,000	Kigali	French, Kinyar–wanda	Rwanda franc	Coffee
São Tomé and Príncipe	387	124,000	São Tomé	Portuguese	Dobra	Cocoa
Senegal	76,124	7,736,000	Dakar	French	Franc CFA	Peanuts, phosphates
Seychelles	108	72,000	Victoria	English, French	Rupee	Copra, fish, spices
Sierra Leone	28,313	4,376,000	Freetown	English	Leone	Diamonds, iron ore
Somali Republic	246,200	9,204,000	Mogadishu	Somali	Somali shilling	Livestock
South Africa	435,047	39,818,000	Pretoria (Government); Cape Town (legal capital)	Afrikaans, English and nine African languages	Rand	Gold, diamonds, fruit, vegetables
Sudan	971,102	26,656,000	Khartoum	Arabic	Sudanese dinar	Cotton, peanuts
Swaziland	6,704	792,000	Mbabane	English	Lilangeni	Sugar, wood pulp, asbestos, fruit
Tanzania	364,880	27,829,000	Dodoma	English, Swahili	Tanzanian shilling	Coffee, cotton, sisal, spices

Country	Area (sq. miles)	Population	Capital	Official language	Currency	Major products
Togo	21,926	3,763,000	Lomé	French	Franc CFA	Phosphates, cocoa, coffee
Tunisia	63,383	8,401,000	Tunis	Arabic	Tunisian dinar	Phosphates, olive oil, oil
Uganda	93,065	18,674,000	Kampala	English	Uganda shilling	Coffee, cotton
Zaire (D.R.C.)	2,345,409	39,882,000	Kinshasa	French	Zaire	Coffee, cobalt, copper
Zambia	290,584	8,638,000	Lusaka	English	Kwacha	Copper
Zimbabwe	150,800	10,583,000	Harare	English	Zimbabwe dollar	Tobacco

Australasia

Facts and Figures

Country	Area (sq. miles)	Population	Capital	Official language	Currency	Major products
Australia	2,967,124	17,529,000	Canberra	English	Australian dollar	Cereals, meat, sugar, honey, fruit, metals and mineral ores, wool
Fiji	7,079	739,000	Suva	English, Fijian	Fiji dollar	Sugar, coconut oil
Kiribati	281	74,000	Tarawa	English, Gilbertese	Australian dollar	Copra, phosphates, fish
Marshall Islands	70	50,000	Majuro	Marshallese, English	US dollar	Copra, sugar, coffee
Micronesia	271	114,000	Palikir	English	US dollar	Fruit, vegetables
Nauru	8	10,000	None	Nauruan, English	Australian dollar	phosphates
New Zealand	104,453	3,414,000	Wellington	English	New Zealand dollar	Meat, dairy products, wool, fruit
Papua New Guinea	178,703	4,056,000	Port Moresby	English	Kina	Copra, cocoa, coffee, copper
Solomon Islands	10,955	342,000	Honiara	English	Solomon Islands dollar	Timber, fish, copra, palm oil
Tonga	289	97,000	Nuku'alofa	English	Paíanga	Copra, bananas
Tuvalu	9	12,000	Fongafala	English, Tuvalu	Australian dollar	Copra
Vanuatu	4,707	157,000	Port Vila	Bislama, English, French	Vatu	Copra, fish
Western Samoa	1,093	158,000	Apia	English, Samoan	Tala	Copra, cocoa, bananas

Index

Page numbers in
italic refer to the
illustrations